Accounting for Managers

Accounting for Managers

Peter M. Bergevin and
Michael M. MacQueen

iUniverse, Inc.
New York   Bloomington

Accounting for Managers

iUniverse books may be ordered through booksellers or by contacting:

iUniverse
1663 Liberty Drive
Bloomington, IN 47403
www.iuniverse.com
1-800-Authors (1-800-288-4677)

ISBN: 978-1-4502-1164-2 (pbk)
ISBN: 978-1-4502-1162-8 (cloth)
ISBN: 978-1-4502-1165-9 (ebk)

Printed in the United States of America

iUniverse rev. date: 5/06/2010

To Linda, Jillian, and Matt Bergevin

To my wife, Leigh, children Sarah and Evan, and my parents

About the Authors

Peter M. Bergevin: Pete Bergevin is a Professor of Accounting at the University of Redlands School of Business where he teaches managerial accounting and financial statement analysis. Prior to his 2004 University of Redlands appointment, Dr. Bergevin chaired Valdosta State's Department of Accounting and Finance for nearly a decade. He also served as an Associate Professor of World Business at Thunderbird—The International Graduate School of Management, and as an Assistant Professor of Accounting at the University of Nevada Las Vegas.

Dr. Bergevin received his PhD in Accounting from Arizona State University. He has published more than seventy-five research manuscripts and cases, which have appeared in such journals as *The CPA Journal, Today's CPA, The Journal of Lending & Credit Risk Management, The Journal of Commercial Bank Lending, The International Executive, Journal of Accounting Education, The Journal of Accounting and Finance Research, Case Research Journal,* and *Business Case Journal.* He has previously published *Financial Statement Analysis: An Integrated Approach* (Prentice Hall) and is completing *The Content and Context of Financial Statement Analysis* (due in 2010).

Dr. Bergevin has lectured in accounting and financial analysis in Mexico, New Zealand, and Europe as well as in the United States. He is an active member of many professional and accounting associations. Dr. Bergevin has served on the editorial board of academic journals and reviews manuscripts for numerous journals and case research organizations. He also provides financial and postretirement benefit consulting to public and private entities as well as serving as an expert legal witness.

In his spare time, Pete enjoys traveling, renovating homes and furniture, reading about history and current events, and following sporting activities.

Michael M. MacQueen: Michael MacQueen is an Assistant Professor of Accounting at the University of Redlands School of Business, where he teaches undergraduate and graduate financial and managerial accounting courses.

Professor MacQueen earned a doctorate in organizational leadership from the University of LaVerne and holds an MBA with an accounting concentration from the California State Polytechnic University, Pomona, and a BA in economics from the University of California, Los Angeles. He is a licensed CPA in the state of California, is an active member of the American Institute of Certified Public Accountants (AICPA), and serves as Audit Committee Chairman for the Inland Empire Chapter of the Institute of Internal Auditors (IIA).

Prior to his appointment at the University of Redlands, Professor MacQueen spent more than twenty years working in a variety of positions in the accounting industry. He served as Audit Manager for the international accounting firm KPMG, as a Corporate Controller of a publicly traded electronics firm, and as Vice President in charge financial audit, taxation, and Sarbanes-Oxley compliance for a large financial institution.

Professor MacQueen is a frequent presenter on accounting, auditing, risk management, and compliance topics. In 2006, he was awarded *Speaker of the Year* by the American Payroll Association (SGV), and he recently appeared on SOX Television, an Internet network that covers issues connected to the Sarbanes-Oxley Act, and the related areas of governance, risk, and compliance.

In his spare time, Mike enjoys travel and outdoor activities, particularly hiking and backpacking. He recently completed climbs of Mt. Whitney and Yosemite's Half Dome.

Contents

Acknowledgments

Numerous people contributed to *Accounting for Managers*. The authors gratefully acknowledge the constructive comments and suggestions made by numerous MBA students at the University of Redlands. We also thank our students for their patient use of the online versions of this text. Their willingness to negotiate the challenges associated with the electronic media made this book possible. Pete and Mike are indebted to Adjunct Professor Janelle Mitchell for using a very early version of this book in her MBA class. We also thank Joanie James and her staff of the School of Business Faculty Support Center at the University of Redlands for their contributions in producing this book. Finally, we offer a big tip of the hat to Vanessa Siliezar at the U of R for her tireless efforts in formatting the final version of the manuscript.

Preface

Welcome to *Accounting for Managers*. We have written this unique introductory text to teach you about the value of accounting information. Your understanding this book's material will improve the quality of the economic decisions that you make on behalf of your organization. It will teach you how to improve your entity's operations, make better investments on its behalf, and lower financing costs.

The authors view accounting as a broad-based financial information system. One cannot understand managerial accounting without comprehending the context that produces such data. Consequently, you will learn about the inputs and processes as well as the outputs of the accounting system in this text. This holistic approach to the subject matter links the organization's accounting system to the outside world. This enables readers to appreciate both the benefits and limitations of financial data. Moreover, a systemic study of accounting produces a valuable additional benefit. People also make a variety of economic decisions outside of their managerial capacity. Foremost among these opportunities are personal investing and lending decisions. Accounting information provides a basis for these decisions, and the information contained in this text will help readers better allocate scarce resources.

We have written *Accounting for Managers* to meet a specific need in the marketplace: a clear, concise, and challenging introduction to accounting. The following three items expand on the text's orientation and the authors underlying philosophy about the subject matter.

- **Orientation**: *Accounting for Managers* is an introductory accounting textbook. It assumes unfamiliarity with the accounting discipline. Our intent is to present an overview of accounting in a direct manner that develops the reader's appreciation and understanding of the role of accounting within the organization and with society as a whole.
- **Scope**: This text is deliberately concise. It addresses the critical aspects of accounting, but it excludes peripheral information that detracts

from its readability and decision focus. Consequently, *Accounting for Managers* is not encyclopedic in nature. Numerous chapter endnotes provide direction for those readers who wish to pursue specific topics in detail. After studying the material in this book, the authors envision a manager who can understand basic accounting data and use it to make rational decisions. We also hope that managers come to appreciate the inherent complexities of financial reporting and know enough to seek expert help when situations warrant it.

- **Assignments**: Readers will find two types of assignments at the end of each chapter: problems and a case study. Befitting the concise nature of this text, end-of-chapter assignments are not numerous. Each one, however, is important to mastering the course material. We have written the problems to reinforce your understanding of the concepts addressed in the chapter. The case study challenges readers to make management decisions based on accounting data. Whereas the problems are straightforward in nature, the cases are less direct. Readers will have to reach conclusions based on the chapter material and make assumptions when solving the cases. Unlike the problems, there may be numerous acceptable answers to a case study. Rigorous analysis and logical conclusions are the two most important factors in writing a good case solution.

We thank you for using this inaugural edition of *Accounting for Managers* and encourage your suggestions for future editions.

Chapter 1

Accounting Information

CHAPTER LEARNING OBJECTIVES

Upon completion of this chapter, readers should be able to:
- ➤ State the objective of accounting.
- ➤ Compare and contrast managerial accounting with financial accounting.
- ➤ Identify the purpose of each of the four financial statements.
- ➤ Integrate the four financial statements into a comprehensive information set.
- ➤ Relate accounting assumptions and principles to financial data.
- ➤ Articulate the primary steps in the accounting process.
- ➤ Implement the dual-entry system of accounting.

Accounting measures and communicates financial information about an entity so that people can make informed economic decisions. Various groups adapt accounting data to meet their specific needs. Accounting information helps the managers of businesses, governmental agencies, and not-for-profit entities operate the organization, secure financing, and prioritize investments. Financial data enables equity investors to project returns on their capital infusions. Lenders use accounting data to forecast the probability of timely debt service.

This text focuses on the relationship between managers and accounting information. As such, it teaches managers how to efficiently access, interpret, and implement accounting data in order to meet the needs of their organizations. In addition, this book examines the unique role that managers play in the accounting information system. As organizational stewards, managers control financial information on behalf of other stakeholders, such as investors. Managers, therefore, must ensure the integrity of accounting data for others who depend upon it. Throughout the text, we explore this unique role by connecting managerial accounting with the larger areas of financial reporting and organizational performance.

Accounting Overview

This first chapter defines accounting, examines the way an entity processes accounting data, presents the output of the accounting system, and discusses its usefulness as a source of information for making economic decisions.

Systems Approach

The accounting department provides organizational stakeholders with financial data about its operating, investing, and financing activities. Its efforts enable the entity to meet its overarching strategic goal: creating wealth by for-profit enterprises or addressing specific societal needs by public and not-for-profit agencies. Managers and other stakeholders use accounting inputs to make a wide range of prudent decisions to help the organization meet its mission.[1]

Convention usually divides the study of the accounting discipline into the areas of managerial and financial accounting. **Managerial accounting** is the accounting sub-discipline that provides monetary informational needs to people within the organization. Good management accounting helps align individual behavior and departmental operations with overall corporate goals.

Managerial accounting is often forward-looking in nature—it quantifies organizational expectations. The accounting system then accumulates actual performance data, which enables managers to compare and contrast those results from their forecasts. Cost measurement and allocation are integral elements in establishing budgets and analyzing departures from them. A good deal of managerial accounting, therefore, concerns itself with the measurement and reporting of costs, which are the economic sacrifices that the entity incurs in order to meet its mission.

Financial accounting, the other broad area of accounting, concentrates on providing economic information to those who have economic interests in the organization, but are not privy to the day-to-day operations of the enterprise. Financial accounting, or external financial reporting, conveys economic data to investors, creditors, and the public. Current and potential shareholders and lenders use such information to determine how they will allocate their limited economic resources in profit-seeking firms. Government entities must account for their actions to their citizens, and other non-profits must report to their donors.

The dichotomization of the study of accounting into managerial and financial subsections is somewhat artificial. Accounting is a single financial information system that facilities a range of economic decisions. The specific decision merely depends on the role of the decision maker. This text covers both internal and external elements of accounting with the goal of improving decision-making capabilities. It assumes no prior knowledge of accounting, only a willingness to understand the value of accounting as a decision-making tool.

One can view accounting from a systems perspective:
A general information system model is as follows:
Inputs → Process → Output → Feedback

Specifically, applying the systems approach to the accounting discipline yields the following model:
Identifying economic events → Compiling financial data → Reporting financial results in statement form → Improving the accounting system

Exhibit 1-1 graphically represents the accounting information system:

EXHIBIT 1-1

ACCOUNTING INFORMATION SYSTEM

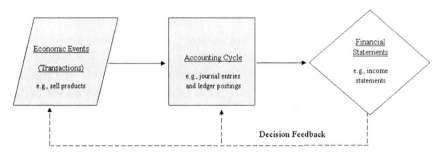

Through their control of the systemic process, managers must ensure the proper functioning of accounting-related data, use that information to plan and control organizational activities, and disclose appropriate financial reports to other stakeholders. Given that the ultimate output of the accounting information system is the financial statements, this becomes a logical place to begin exploring the value of accounting to the organization and to broader aspects of society.

We will now briefly identify each of the four financial statements, discuss the objective for each one, and define the major elements.

FINANCIAL STATEMENTS

Organizations report four distinct **financial statements** that present the results of economic activity. The specific names of these statements may vary, depending on whether the organization seeks profits or is a non-profit entity. (The following financial statement titles assume a for-profit enterprise. Chapter 2 will discuss alternative financial statement headings in the not-for-profit realm.)

- **Balance Sheet**—reports an entity's financial position at a single point in time, such as the last day of the business year. It equates a firm's **assets** (economic resources) to the sum of its **liabilities** (economic obligations to non-owners) and **shareholders' equity** (owners' interest in the business). More succinctly:

  Assets = Liabilities + Shareholders' Equity

  Rearranging the balance sheet equation emphasizes the owners' interest in the enterprise: assets – liabilities = shareholders' equity. This approach demonstrates that the owners' interest equals the entity's net assets.[2]

- **Statement of Shareholders' Equity**—discloses the changes in the owners' business interest over time (such as one year). Owners' equity increases when the business operates profitably or when stockholders inject capital into the enterprise. Their net assets decrease when the company declares a cash dividend or when the entity acquires its own stock in the secondary equity markets.

- **Income Statement**—reports the results of business operations over time. These operations are captured in the following income statement equation:

  Revenues – Expenses = Net Income (or profit or earnings)

Companies recognize **revenues** by selling goods or providing services to customers. **Expenses**, in turn, are the entity's business costs incurred in generating those revenues. Net income, or the difference between revenues and expenses, equals the wealth created by a business during the reporting period.[3]

- **Statement of Cash Flows**—reports the net increase or decrease in cash during a reporting period. The change in this asset, or economic resource, results from three distinct types of business activities. This statement discloses the inflow and outflow of cash from operating, investing, and financing activities.

INTERRELATIONSHIP OF FINANCIAL STATEMENTS

Each of the above financial statements reports a specific type of economic activity (such as the balance sheet reporting the organization's financial position). The same underlying transactions, however, can affect all four financial statements. Each financial statement merely captures certain aspects of those transactions. Consequently, the manager must consider all four financial statements as an integrated set of information rather than as separate sources of financial data. Exhibit 1-2 graphically presents the interrelated nature of the financial statements.

Exhibit 1-2
Articulated Financial Statements

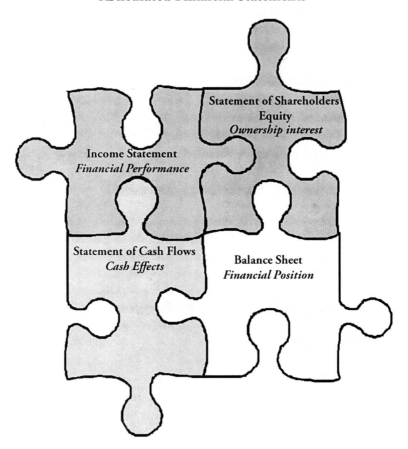

GENERALLY ACCEPTED ACCOUNTING PRINCIPLES

Authoritative pronouncements and accepted conventions influence financial statement disclosures and provide common ground for using accounting data. Managers must understand these **generally accepted accounting principles (GAAP)** and their theoretical underpinnings in order to appreciate financial data compilation and financial statement disclosures.

Reporting Standards

Financial statement principles provide a basis for measuring, valuing, and comparing economic activity. These standards provide consistent disclosure over time, and permit meaningful comparisons among companies. Commercial, economic, legal, cultural, social, political, and educational factors all influence the development of these standards. Evolution yielded some principles; policy created others. Moreover, reporting principles change as business practices and user needs shift. Managers need to remember that financial reporting standards are human contrivances, rather than immutable laws of nature.

A working relationship between the public and private sectors determines the authoritative standards that constitute GAAP in the United States. The federal government's **Securities and Exchange Commission (SEC)** has legal authority to set accounting standards, but it has generally ceded that task to a private organization, the **Financial Accounting Standards Board (FASB)**.[4] The SEC reviews GAAP as part of its regulatory responsibilities and the commission often influences the FASB by taking a position on unresolved financial reporting issues. The collaborative efforts of the SEC and FASB have produced many accounting principles and rules that constitute the backbone of financial reporting.

Reporting standards affect corporate profitability and financial position; consequently, many of these pronouncements are quite controversial. However, despite some dissatisfaction, the public/private partnership generally succeeds in producing timely and detailed financial reporting standards. These rules improve capital market efficiency, or the allocation of economic resources.

GAAP currently varies throughout the world, but the trend is toward standardization. Many countries now require firms to conform to a global set of principles, promulgated by the **International Accounting Standards Board (IASB)**.[5] It is unlikely that this international set of standards will replace U.S. GAAP as the primary American financial reporting authority in the near term. The FASB views itself as the premier standard-setting body in the world, the one that has produced the best set of in-depth financial reporting standards.[6] In many instances, however, the IASB and FASB work closely together to improve financial reporting. These joint ventures have led to more comparable financial statements between U.S. and foreign firms.

ASSUMPTIONS

Standards setting bodies seek to enact rules of accounting that comport to economic reality. Therefore, underlying assumptions and principles govern financial disclosures. The first assumption is that financial disclosures represent a specific economic entity. This **economic entity assumption** means that a corporation is an independent, separate, and distinct entity from its owners. As a separate concern, managers must report only the firm's economic activities; they do not report non-entity owner resources, obligations, and wealth. In addition, GAAP requires that a firm report its economic substance, rather than its legal form. Therefore, a company with numerous legally distinct corporations reports only one set of financial statements, called **consolidated financial statements**, to the outside world.

Exhibit 1-3 lists four other assumptions that also influence financial statement reporting:[7]

Exhibit 1-3
Primary Financial Reporting Assumptions

Assumption	Definition
Periodicity	A company discloses its financial statements on a regular, recurring basis (e.g., annually or quarterly).
Going concern	An entity will continue operating indefinitely into the future.
Monetary unit	A firm reports all financial statement accounts in terms of currency (i.e., dollars for U.S. firms).
Stable dollar	An enterprise does not adjust its financial statements for changes in general price levels (inflation) or specific-item amounts (physical units).

The four assumptions listed above provide the manager with the appropriate lens with which to view the general-purpose financial reporting system. Managers understand that the economic entity, periodicity, going concern, monetary unit, and stable dollar assumptions anchor financial statement disclosures, regardless of one's reason for analyzing the financial statements.

PRINCIPLES

Companies record transactions at historical exchange prices and those historical costs tend to serve as the valuation basis on the financial statements.[8] Firms also base financial statements on **accrual accounting**, which reflects the cash consequences of business events. Generally accepted accounting principles mandate accrual basis accounting, as opposed to its reporting alternative—cash basis accounting. This latter non-GAAP method recognizes revenues upon receipt of cash and expenses when paid in cash.

Two principles govern accrual accounting. The **revenue recognition principle** dictates when revenue is recognized and reported in the income statement.[9] In general, a firm recognizes revenue and reports it on the income statement when it exchanges goods or services for cash or claims to cash (commonly called accounts receivable).[10] Its complement, the **matching principle**, deducts the costs of generating those revenues to determine income for a reporting period. Another way to view the matching principle is that companies record specific costs, called expenses, as incurred, regardless of when the cash is actually paid.

Remember, accrual accounting differs from the cash basis of accounting. Entities recognize revenues as earned and match expenses as incurred; the difference between these two constructs is income. Income does not equal the net amount of cash receipts minus cash payments.

ACCOUNTING PROCESS

Managers must understand how an entity processes economic data to appreciate the information content of accounting. The final section of this introductory chapter explores the primary steps in the **accounting cycle**. Five key steps in this process or cycle are as follows:

1. Recording journal entries
2. Posting to the ledger
3. Constructing a trial balance
4. Presenting the financial statements
5. Closing the temporary accounts

One must understand the **dual-entry system of accounting** in order to prepare and record journal entries. The dual-entry system means that every transaction maintains the integrity of the balance sheet. This means that the three elements of the balance sheet (assets, liabilities, and shareholders' equity) remain in balance at all times: assets = liabilities + shareholders' equity. Entities make **journal entries** by recording increases and decreases to specific accounts. An **account** is a specific type of element. For example, cash is an asset account and salaries payable is a liability account.

The dual-entry system records all increases in assets on the left-hand side of the journal (the book of original entry). Accountants refer to the left side of an accounting entry as a **debit**. Conversely, one records a decrease in an asset account by a **credit**. In accounting, the term credit means to record on the right-hand side of an accounting document. The two elements on the other side of the balance sheet equation (liabilities and equity) behave in the opposite manner. One credits specific liability and equity accounts to report an increase in them, and debits liability and equity accounts when they decrease. In order to insure the integrity of the balance sheet equation, the dollar amount of debits must equal the dollar amount of credits for each journal entry.

Two elements compose the income statement: revenues and expenses. These two elements affect shareholders' equity by increasing (or decreasing) net income. Consequently, the accounting system applies dual-entry accounting to income statement accounts. Recall that revenues increase net income, which in turn increases shareholders' wealth. Therefore, one credits revenue when earned. Inasmuch as expenses reduce profitability (and shareholders' equity), the system requires a debit to an expense when the entity incurs it.

JOURNALS

Firms initially report economic transactions in a document (i.e., book or software application) called a **general journal**.[11] For example, assume that Redlands, Inc. issued 10 shares of stock at $1 each to begin its corporate operations on January 1, 2010. The journal entry is as follows:

General Journal

Date	Accounts	Debit	Credit
1/1/10	Cash (an asset account)	10	
	Common stock (a shareholders' equity account)		10

Redlands then earns, but does not collect, $3 in cash by providing consulting services in January. In addition, the firm pays $2 in cash to cover that month's operating expenses. The company records these transactions as follows:

General Journal

Date	Accounts	Debit	Credit
Jan. ---	Accounts receivable	3	
	Service revenue		3
Jan. ---	Operating expenses	2	
	Cash		2

LEDGERS

The journal chronologically lists all transactions, irrespective of the accounts involved in those transactions. Consequently, the accounting system must gather the effects of all transactions on each account in one place in order to understand its monetary balance. Accountants call this document a **ledger**. We post the above transactions to the ledger as follows:

Ledger

Account	Date	Debit	Credit	Balance
Cash	1/1/10	10		10 (debit)
	Jan. ---		2	8 (debit)

Account	Date	Debit	Credit	Balance
Common stock	1/1/10		10	10 (credit)

Account	Date	Debit	Credit	Balance
Service revenue	Jan. ---		10	10 (credit)

Account	Date	Debit	Credit	Balance
Accounts rec.	Jan. ---	10		10 (debit)

Account	Date	Debit	Credit	Balance
Operating exp.	Jan.---	2		2 (debit)

A simpler and commonly used type of ledger is a collection of **T-accounts**. As the name implies, a T-account lists an account with a vertical line drawn underneath it. The accountant records debits to the left of the vertical line and credits to the right of it. The T-account's balance is the difference between the sum of the debits and the sum of the credits.

TRIAL BALANCES

Given the numerous transactions that occur during a reporting period, the system compiles a **trial balance** at the end of the reporting period. The trial balance lists each account's ending monetary balance. The trial balance for Redlands is as follows:

Trial Balance

Accounts	Debit	Credit
Cash	$8	
Common stock		$10
Sales revenue		3
Accounts receivable	3	
Operating expenses	2	
Totals	**$13**	**$13**

FINANCIAL STATEMENTS

One sorts the accounts on the trial balance into financial statements, beginning with the income statement. We illustrate Redlands financial statements as follows:

Redlands, Inc.
Income Statement
For Month Ended January 31, 2010

Revenues	$3
Expenses	2
Net income	$1

Redlands, Inc.
Statement of Shareholders' Equity
For Month Ended January 31, 2010

Beginning shareholders' equity	$ 0
+ Capital invested	10
+ Earnings retained	1
Ending shareholders' equity	$11

Redlands, Inc.
Balance Sheet
At January 31, 2010

Assets:	
Cash	$ 8
Accounts receivable	3
Total assets	$11
Liabilities:	$ 0

Shareholders' Equity:
Common stock	10
Retained earnings	1
Total liabilities and shareholders' equity	$11

Redlands, Inc.
Statement of Cash Flows
For Month Ended January 31, 2010

Cash flows from operating activities:
Cash collected from customers	$ 0
Cash paid for expenses	(2)
Cash flows from operating activities	(2)
Cash flows from investing activities:	0
Cash flows from financing activities:	
Sale of stock	10
Net increase in cash for January	$ 8
Cash balance—January 1, 2010	0
Cash balance—January 31, 2010	$ 8

CLOSING

Note that the retained earnings account, listed in the statement of stockholders' equity and the balance sheet, does not exist in the journal (or the ledger or trial balance for that matter). It is a necessary account, however, to make the balance sheet balance (i.e., assets = liabilities + shareholders' equity). Retained earnings formally arise from the **closing process** of the accounting system. This process accomplishes two goals:

1. to close out or eliminate the ending balances of the temporary (or income statement) accounts
2. to transfer net income (or net loss) to retained earnings

The accountant closes out income statement accounts (revenues and expenses) in order to avoid double-counting revenues and expenses in the next reporting period. The system does not close the balance sheet, or permanent accounts, because the ending balance for one period becomes the beginning balance in the next one. Notice how the firm will have $8 of cash and $3 of accounts receivable when it begins operations in February.

Redlands makes the following closing entries for January 2010:

Date	Accounts	Debit	Credit
1/31/10	Service revenue	3	
	Retained earnings		3
1/31/10	Retained earnings	2	
	Operating expenses		2

Notice that retained earnings results in a $1 credit balance from the two closing entries.

Summary

This chapter defined accounting, examined the accounting process, and evaluated the output of the accounting system—the financial statements. This chapter addressed the holistic nature of accounting information and focused on its contributions to rational economic decision-making. Managers learned the means by which the entity processes data in this chapter. By studying the material, managers also became aware of the integrated nature of financial disclosures through the process of articulation.

Key Terms

Account
Accounting
Accounting cycle
Accrual accounting
Articulation
Assets
Balance sheet
Closing process
Consolidated financial statements
Credit
Debit
Dual-entry system of accounting
Economic entity assumption
Expenses
Financial accounting
Financial Accounting Standards Board (FASB)
Financial statements
General journal
Generally accepted accounting principles (GAAP)
Going concern
Income statement
International Accounting Standards Board (IASB)
Journal entries
Ledger
Liabilities
Managerial accounting
Matching principle
Monetary unit
Periodicity
Retained earnings
Revenue recognition principle
Revenues
Securities Exchange Commission (SEC)
Shareholders' equity
Stable monetary unit
Statement of cash flows
Trial balance

Assignments

Accounting Concepts Crossword

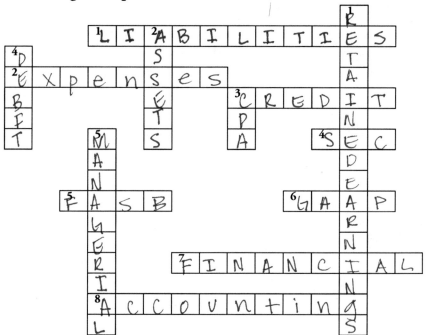

Across	**Down**

Across

[1] Probable future sacrifices of economic benefits arising from present obligations (economic obligations to non-owners).

[2] Outflows or other using up of assets or incurring of liabilities during a period.

[3] An entry on the right side of an account.

[4] Independent regulatory agency of the U.S. government that provides oversight in the establishment of accounting standards for publically traded companies.

[5] Private, independent board which issues accounting pronouncements.

[6] Accounting principles that have substantial authoritative support.

[7] Area of accounting that deals with providing information primarily for users external to the organization.

[8] The art of recording, classifying, and summarizing in a significant manner and in terms of money, transactions, and events that is of financial character, and interpreting the results thereof.

Down

[1] The portion of net income, which is retained by the corporation rather than distributed to its owners as dividends.

[2] Probable future economic benefits obtained or resources controlled by an organization (resources).

[3] The statutory title of accountants in the U.S. who have passed a uniform exam and satisfied other state licensing requirements.

[4] An entry on the left side of an account.

[5] Area of accounting that deals with providing information primarily for users internal to the organization.

DISCUSSION ITEMS

What Would Your Accountant Say?

The president of your company has asked the controller to give the members of your department a brief overview of the elements in the basic accounting equation (assets = liabilities + equity), including a description of each element and a sample of the accounts that might be contained within each element. At the last minute, someone calls the controller away and the president, knowing you are taking an accounting course as part of your MBA program, has asked you to fill in. What would your accountant say to the department?

Theory vs. Practice

Accountants have established procedures for recording, classifying, summarizing, and reporting financial transactions. They commonly refer to these procedures as the *accounting cycle*. This chapter condenses the accounting cycle into five key steps; however, in theory, a manual accounting system might include all of the following:

1. Identification and analysis of transactions (analyzing)
2. Entering the transactions in appropriate journals (journalizing)
3. Posting from the journals to the ledger (posting)
4. Preparing an unadjusted trial balance (first trial)
5. Preparing adjusting journal entries (adjusting)
6. Preparing and adjusted trial balance (second trial)
7. Preparing the financial statements
8. Preparing closing entries (closing)
9. Preparing a post-closing trial balance (third trial)

In practice, a computerized accounting system could perform many of these steps automatically. Discuss which of the steps in the accounting cycle listed above that you believe might be performed by a computer, versus those that would need to be performed manually by an accountant, and explain your reasoning.

PROBLEMS

Problem 1-1

Blacklands, Inc. has the following transactions during 2010, its first year of business:

   a. Sells $160 of stock to begin operations on January 1.
   b. Borrows $200 from a bank on January 1. Blacklands signs a note with the bank agreeing to pay 10% interest annually on December 31 and to repay the principal on December 31, 2012.
   c. Pays annual rent of $40 on January 1, 2010 (establish prepaid rent as an asset).
   d. Purchases $100 of inventory on January 2 on credit.
   e. Pays its vendor for the inventory on February 1.
   f. Purchases equipment costing $120 on July 1. The company expects the equipment to last 6 years.
   g. Makes $225 of sales during 2010. One third of the sales are in cash and the other two-thirds are on credit.
   h. Records the $90 cost of inventory used to make the sales in letter g above.
   i. Collects one third of the credit sales in cash on December 29.
   j. Incurs, but does not pay, $60 of salaries for 2010 (recorded on December 31).
   k. Records the using up of prepaid rent (letter c above) at December 31.
   l. Depreciates the equipment for one half of a year on December 31.
   m. Pays the accrued interest on the note (letter b above).

Blacklands uses the following chart of accounts to record its transactions:

Assets	Liabilities	S/Equity	Revenues	Expenses
101 Cash	201 Accounts payable	301 Common stock	401 Sales revenue	501 Cost of goods sold
102 Accounts receivable	202 Notes payable			502 Salaries expense
103 Inventory	203 Salaries payable			503 Rent expense
104 Prepaid rent				504 Depreciation expense
105 Equipment				505 Interest expense
106 Accumulated depreciation (a reduction of the equipment account)				

Required: Use the chart of accounts above to process transactions a through m. Complete the following:

1. Record the journal entries
2. Post to the ledger
3. Construct the trial balance
4. Present the financial statements (exclude the statement of cash flows)
5. Close the temporary accounts and transfer income to retained earnings

Problem 1-2

Given the following data from the Coca-Cola Company (amounts in millions of dollars):

Income Statement	2007	
Revenues	$28,857	
Expenses	20,984	
Pretax income	7,873	
Income tax expenses	1,892	
Net income	$ 5,981	

Balance Sheets	2007	2006
Cash and cash equivalents		$ 2,440
All other assets	39,176	27,523
Total assets		29,963
Total liabilities	21,525	13,043
Total shareholders' equity	21,744	16,920
Total liabilities and shareholders' equity		$29,963

Statement of Cash Flows	2007	
Cash flows from operating activities	$7,150	
Cash flows from investing activities	(6,719)	
Cash flows from financing activities	1,222	
Net increase in cash	$1,653	

Required: Determine the following missing 2007 financial statement amounts:

1. Total liabilities and shareholders' equity
2. Total assets
3. Cash and cash equivalents (using 2007 balance sheet data)
4. Cash and cash equivalents (using 2006 cash balance and 2007 statement of cash flows data)

CASE 1-1

You are the new chief financial officer for Redlands Manufacturing, Inc. The firm that you have just joined has recently paid substantial penalties to settle claims related to fraudulent financial reporting practices. The board of directors has also created an Office of Ethics and Compliance in response to the scandals. Francis Bacon, the chief of the newly created ethics office, recently dropped by your office for some insights about accounting and fraudulent financial reporting.

The chief ethicist stated that he has a background in philosophy, but he lacks understanding of the accounting discipline. He identifies the tactics that the company employed when it essentially *cooked its books*. Bacon stated that Redlands employed some devious practices that were obviously unethical, but that he lacked the accounting vocabulary to articulate their financial statement consequences. He essentially wanted to understand why specific practices violated accounting standards and sought your help with this matter.

Bacon began by stating, "I have identified five types of arrangements that Redlands engaged in over the period in question. Each type of activity has a clever sounding name. Here is my list":

Channel Stuffing. Redlands shipped manufactured goods to certain retailers in certain instances regardless of whether or not the retailers ordered the products. Our firm recognized revenues upon shipment of these non-ordered items, which usually took place toward the end of the year. We informally agreed to take back the merchandise if the retailer could not sell it. It was kind of a wink and a nod deal. Redlands did not recognize an allowance for the merchandise that its retailers could return.

Vendor Dinging. Redlands told many of its suppliers that the company received a disproportionately large number of raw materials that did not conform to contracted specifications. Consequently, Redlands unilaterally decreased its cash payments to those vendors. Most of the suppliers did not dispute Redlands claims and merely reduced Redlands obligation to them. Of course, many of those materials were of acceptable quality and we used them in manufacturing our products.

Capitalizing Revenue Expenditures. Redlands placed numerous recurring business costs on its balance sheet as long-term assets, rather than charging the full cost of the item as an expense in the current reporting period. Redlands then recognized only a portion of those questionable assets' costs as a current expense, which the company called depreciation. These costs, such as salaries expense, had no future benefit beyond the current reporting period.

Special Purpose Entities (SPEs). Redlands Manufacturing shielded debt (liabilities) from its balance sheet with these types of arrangements. Redlands contracted with ostensibly independent companies in business ventures that were debt financed. The other companies, not Redlands, reported the debt on their balance sheets. The SPE partners, however, consisted of businesses established by Redlands executives.

Round Tripping. Redlands provided its products to advertising firms in exchange for newspaper, Internet, television, and radio ads. In these exchanges, Redlands and its trading partners (the advertising firms) would recognize revenues, but they would not record any business expenses related to the deals.

Imagine that Bacon told you that he was preparing to make his initial address to the board of directors concerning staff training, which should assure that the firm does not engage in any of the above or similar practices. He asks that you explain to him how such unethical practices violate accounting conventions, and how they inflated the financial appearance of the firm.

Required. Write a memorandum to Francis Bacon explaining how each practice violated generally accepted accounting principles and how each type of transaction affected reported income, financial position, and cash flows.

Endnotes

1   This text generally assumes for-profit corporations as its default type of organization. Chapter 2 relaxes this assumption in its evaluation of accounting in the not-for-profit sector.

2   We use the term owners' interest rather than owners' wealth, because the balance sheet often does not accurately measure the common notion of equity, which is the market value of the owners' stock.

3   Generally accepted accounting principles define wealth creation this way.

4   Accounting Series Release No. 150 of the SEC, *Statement of Policy on the Establishment and Improvement of Accounting Rules,* effectively yielded financial reporting standard setting to the Financial Accounting Standards Board (FASB).

5   The European Union requires all companies domiciled within its member nations to conform to international accounting standards.

6   A philosophical difference exists between the FASB and IASB. American accounting standards contain detailed rules, whereas international ones focus more on general reporting principles.

7   Exhibit 1-3 highlights some of the key aspects affecting accounting. Technically, more numerous assumptions, principles, and constraints affect financial reporting disclosures.

8   We discuss exceptions to this general principle throughout the text.

9   We use revenue realization and revenue recognition interchangeably in this text. A technical difference exceeds the scope of this text.

10 This discussion presumes the reporting entity has *earned* the revenue (i.e., it did everything it has to do to earn the benefits resulting from the revenues). In addition, revenue can be *realizable,* rather than realized. In this instance, a company can convert assets into cash or claims to cash.

11 Actual accounting systems contain numerous journals dedicated to specific events, such as purchases. We assume only a general journal to facilitate understanding of the process.

Chapter 2

Accounting Disclosures

CHAPTER LEARNING OBJECTIVES

Upon completion of this chapter, readers should be able to:
- ➤ Distinguish between the financial reporting objectives of for-profit and not-for-profit organizations.
- ➤ Understand the detailed composition of each of the four financial statements.
- ➤ Analyze how financial statements interrelate with one another in order to provide useful information to managers, investors, and creditors.
- ➤ Adapt financial statement disclosures to reflect the informational needs of governmental and voluntary agencies.
- ➤ Synthesize the role of funds into a governmental accounting system.

An accounting system measures and communicates financial information in order to help make prudent, economic decisions. As we noted in Chapter 1, the financial statements are the output of an accounting system. Managers must be able to understand and analyze the organization's financial scorecard in order to assess past performance and to forecast future activities. The first section of this chapter explores the composition and interrelationships among the four financial statements in detail. The second half of the chapter explores the unique financial reporting disclosures of not-for-profit entities. Inasmuch as the fundamental goal of not-for-profit organizations is to serve a particular segment of society, rather than to create wealth, these organizations' financial statements must provide their managers with mission-specific information.

All accounting systems share certain similarities in the way that they process information (e.g., journal entries and ledgers); however, specific aspects of the accounting function result from organizational need. Such differences are evident even among for-profit firms. For example, a retailer may account for all of its transactions with its suppliers of inventory in a distinct *purchases* journal. The accounting system of a service firm, on the other hand, would not need such a journal. Merchants match the cost of inventory sold against revenues earned in a reporting period, and they disclose unsold inventory on their balance sheets. Conversely, a service firm would not report such an expense or asset on its financial statements, because it does not buy or sell tangible goods. Regardless of the specific accounting processes, however, all profit-seeking firms disclose four financial statements. We introduced these statements in the first chapter and now examine the reports in detail.

COMPREHENSIVE DISCLOSURES

Recall that general-purpose financial reports consist of four specific financial statements, which we quantitatively illustrated in the Chapter 1 Redlands example. To reiterate, the four financial statements are the:

1. income statement
2. statement of shareholders' equity
3. balance sheet
4. statement of cash flows

These statements respectively disclose operating performance, ownership interest, financial position, and cash sources and uses. This section more explicitly defines the objective, identifies terms, and presents the format for each financial statement. It also introduces a hypothetical Internet entity, Extreme Edge, Inc., in order to illustrate financial statement content and composition. We will continue to use financial statement data from this fictitious start-up firm when addressing other issues at later points in the text.

BUSINESS START-UP

A group of recent college graduates decided to form their own business, rather than work for someone else. These aspiring entrepreneurs perceived a market niche for extreme sports equipment, especially those items not stocked by traditional sporting goods retailers. These budding businesspeople did not want to open a storefront because they lacked capital, sought broader market penetration, and perceived a more efficient distribution channel. As a result, they founded Extreme Edge, Inc. an Internet retailer.

The company's first balance sheet, or statement of financial position, resulted from its corporate financing activities. The entity's initial assets consisted of invested cash. Two claims existed against that cash. The entrepreneurs and venture capitalists' interest in the resources constituted initial shareholders' equity.[1] The sole obligation to non-owners, on the other hand, was money borrowed from a bank. The company then used some of its cash to acquire other assets, such as inventory and computer equipment. Extreme Edge captured those transactions in its accounting system and maintained the integrity of the balance sheet equation: **assets = liabilities + shareholders' equity**.

Like all profit-seeking businesses, the owners of Extreme Edge want to maximize their wealth. To that end, the company sells merchandise at historical cost plus a retail markup. The income statement reports the results of its wealth-seeking activities. The equation (**revenues − expenses = net income**) reports Extreme Edge's ability to produce wealth over a specified interval of time.

Assuming Extreme Edge earns income, it can keep the entire profit in the business, distribute it all to the owners, or retain a portion and pay out the rest.[2] **Retained earnings** are undistributed profits, whereas **dividends** equal payments to shareholders. Income-related decisions capture the most important aspect of the statement of shareholders' equity. This statement, in essence, reports **beginning shareholders' equity + net income − dividends = ending shareholders' equity**.[3] Another way to view the primary portion of the statement of shareholders' equity is as a bridge connecting the income statement to the balance sheet. It links the two statements because the income statement measures wealth changes over time, and the balance sheets bracket that income statement disclosure with the beginning and ending amounts of income retained in the business.

The ending balance in shareholders' equity also increases when the firm sells stock to shareholders. Inasmuch as Extreme Edge began operations in 2008, its shareholders' equity statement for that year reported changes in **contributed capital**, or the owners' investment in the firm. Companies can also reduce capital contributions. If, for example, Extreme Edge were to purchase some of its own stock in a secondary market, its number of outstanding shares (and related dollar amount) would decrease.[4]

All corporate stakeholders require information about the amount and timing of cash flows. We have already discussed that accrual basis accounting reports events having cash consequences, as opposed to focusing on just the cash flowing into and out of an organization. As noted in Chapter 1, revenues and expenses do not equal cash inflows and outflows. For example, assume Extreme Edge made a number of 2008 sales that went uncollected until the next year. Those 2008 sales created cash consequences, but their 2009 collections produced actual cash. The fourth financial statement compensates for the limitation that accrual accounting tends to give short shrift to cash changes over time. The statement of cash flows reports the net change in cash during a reporting period.

Three distinct activities—operating, investing, and financing—compose the statement of cash flows. Extreme Edge receives cash when it collects on sales, and it uses cash when it pays for merchandise in the normal course of business. The statement of cash flows reports these events as cash flows from operating activities (CFOs). The company used cash provided by owners and creditors to acquire the equipment necessary to run the business. Such cash flows from investing activities (CFIs) constitute the second section of a cash flows statement. Extreme Edge generated cash flows from financing activities (CFFs), which is the third segment of the financial statement, when it sold stock and borrowed money from the bank to launch the business.

Exhibit 2-1 presents Extreme Edge's financial statements for its first four years of business in spreadsheet format.[5]

Exhibit 2-1
Financial Statements—Extreme Edge, Inc.

Income Statements	For the Year Ending December 31			
	(in thousands, except EPS)			
	2011	2010	2009	2008
Sales revenues	$ 1,310	$ 1,240	$ 1,200	$ 1,000
Cost of goods sold	800	719	660	600
Gross profit	510	521	540	400
Selling expenses	355	312	352	250
Administrative expenses	150	150	133	85
Income from continuing operations	5	59	55	65
Interest (financial) expense	20	20	20	10
Pretax income (loss)	(15)	39	35	55
Income tax expense (benefit)	(6)	16	14	22
Net income (loss)	(9)	23	21	33
Earnings (loss) per share	(0.18)	0.46	0.42	0.79

Statements of Stockholders' Equity (in thousands, except par value)	Common Stock	Additional PIC	Retained Earnings
Balance as of January 1, 2008	$ -	$ -	$ -
Common stock issued, $1 par value	42	378	-
Net income	-	-	33
Dividends declared and paid	-	-	(8)
Balance as of December 31, 2008	$ 42	$ 378	$ 25
Balance as of January 1, 2009	$ 42	$ 378	$ 25
Common stock issued, $1 par value	8	72	-
Net income	-	-	21
Dividends declared and paid	-	-	(2)
Balance as of December 31, 2009	$ 50	$ 450	$ 44
Balance as of January 1, 2010	$ 50	$ 450	$ 44
Common stock issued, $1 par value	-	-	-
Net income	-	-	23
Dividends declared and paid	-	-	(2)
Balance as of December 31, 2010	$ 50	$ 450	$ 65
Balance as of January 1, 2011	$ 50	$ 450	$ 65
Common stock issued, $1 par value	-	-	-
Net income (loss)	-	-	(9)
Dividends declared and paid	-	-	-
Balance as of December 31, 2011	$ 50	$ 450	$ 56

Balance Sheets (as of December 31)							
(in thousands of dollars)	**2011**		**2010**		**2009**		**2008**
Assets							
Current assets:							
Cash	$	34	$	187	$	45	$ 30
Short-term investments		60		-		-	-
Accounts receivable, net		160		175		140	120
Inventory		335		270		250	200
Prepaid expenses		8		12		5	10
Total current assets		597		644		440	360
Property, plant, and equipment:							
Equipment, net		204		260		380	400
Intangible assets:							
Customer database, net		5		10		15	20
Total Assets	$	806	$	914	$	835	$ 780
Liabilities							
Current liabilities:							
Accounts payable	$	110	$	80	$	50	$ 160
Accrued liabilities		40		43		21	50
Income taxes payable		=		6		=	5
Total current liabilities		150		129		71	215
Long-term liabilities:							

(handwritten) Patents, copyrights — next to "Intangible assets:"

(handwritten) salaries, utilities, Advertising — next to "Accrued liabilities"

(handwritten) ⌐ Dont require a cash payment within a year

Notes payable	100	220	220	120
Total Liabilities	250	349	291	335
Shareholders' Equity				
Common stock, $1 par	50	50	50	42
Additional paid-in-capital on common stock	450	450	450	378
Total contributed capital	500	500	500	420
Retained earnings	56	65	44	25
Total shareholders' equity	556	565	544	445
Total Liabilities and Shareholders' Equity	$ 806	$ 914	$ 835	$ 780

| Statements of Cash Flows | For the Year Ending December 31 | | | |
(in thousands of dollars)	2011	2010	2009	2008
Cash flows from operating activities:				
Net income (loss)	$ (9)	$ 23	$ 21	$ 33
Depreciation expense, equipment	136	120	120	100
Amortization expense, customer database (Non Cash Item)	5	5	5	5
Changes in current accounts:				
Accounts receivable	15	(35)	(20)	(120)
Inventory	(65)	(20)	(50)	(200)
Prepaid expenses	4	(7)	5	(10)
Accounts payable	30	30	(110)	160
Accrued liabilities	(3)	22	(29)	50
Taxes payable	(6)	6	(5)	5
Net cash provided by (used in) operating activities	107	144	(63)	23
Cash flows from investing activities:				
Purchase of equipment	(80)	-	(100)	(500)
Acquisition of customer database	-	-	-	(25)
Purchase of short-term investments	(60)	-	-	-
Net cash provided by (used in) investing activities	(140)	-	(100)	(525)
Cash flows from financing activities:				
Issue (retire) notes payable	(120)	-	100	120
Issue common stock	-	-	80	420

Pay cash dividend	=	(2)	(2)	(8)
Net cash provided by (used in) financing activities	(120)	(2)	178	532
Net change in cash	$ (153)	$ 142	$ 15	$ 30
Cash, beginning of the year	$ 187	$ 45	$ 30	$ -
Cash, end of the year	$ 34	$ 187	$ 45	$ 30

Our discussion of the financial statement disclosures will be limited to 2008 and 2009, the first two years of operations. (Data for the last two years serve as inputs for Problem 2-1 at the end of the chapter.)

INCOME STATEMENT

Companies also refer to the income statement as a *statement of earnings, statement of operating performance, profit and loss statement,* or *P&L statement.* Regardless of the title, the statement reports corporate profitability (or loss, if expenses exceed revenues) over a period of time. Extreme Edge, for instance, earned $33,000 in its first business year (2008) and $21,000 in its second business year (2009). (Note that the spreadsheet data reports monetary amounts in thousands of dollars.) Alternatively, the company earned $.79 and $.42 per share of stock, respectively, in those two periods.

The income statement consists of four parts: revenues, expenses, income or loss, and earnings per share. As mentioned in the last chapter's discussion of the revenue realization principle, revenues increase assets or settle liabilities through selling goods and rendering services. Sales or services constitute an entity's central business activity. In our example, Extreme Edge earns revenues by selling sporting goods over the Internet. **Gains** are like revenues, except they arise from peripheral or incidental transactions.[6] The Internet retailer did not have any gains in its first two years of operations.

Expenses are the cost of doing business, or the resources consumed to make sales or provide services. They decrease assets or increase liabilities. Our hypothetical Internet retailer classified expenses into four categories: costs of goods sold, selling and administrative expenses, interest (or financial) expense, and income tax expense.[7] Peripheral or incidental costs result in **losses**, rather than expenses. No losses occurred for Extreme Edge in either 2008 or 2009. Revenues and gains less expenses and losses equal net income or the change in wealth over a specified time interval, such as one year.[8]

Many income categories exist, as evidenced by Extreme Edge's income statements. Income statements report profit before or after operating expenses, and before or after income taxes. Managers focus on earnings levels per share, instead of aggregate amounts of income. **Earnings per share (EPS)** describe that prorated income disclosure. It reports the amount of net income, or another measure of income, earned by each share of stock during a reporting period. In this case, shareholders held 42,000 and 50,000 shares of Extreme Edge common stock in 2008 and 2009, respectively. We noted EPS amounts ($.79 and $.42) at the beginning of our income statement discussion. Extreme Edge computed them as follows:[9]

$$2008: \$33,000 \ / \ 42,000 \text{ shares} = \$.79$$
$$2009: \$21,000 \ / \ 50,000 \text{ shares} = \$.42$$

The various income categories mentioned above result from Extreme Edge's income statement method. As noted, the Internet firm reported four expense categories, each of which resulted in a measure of profit (e.g., gross profit, income from continuing operations, pretax income, and net income). Managers refer to this type of disclosure as a **multiple-step income statement**. Conversely, a **single-step income statement** reports all categories of revenues and gains, and then subtracts all expenses and losses to determine pretax income. While GAAP allows either method, managers find the multiple-step format more informative and often recast single-step income statements into multiple-step statements.

Cost of goods sold (cost of sales) is the historical cost of inventory sold during a reporting period. Merchants and manufacturers deduct their cost of sales from sales revenues to determine **gross profit (gross margin** or **gross profit margin)**. Extreme Edge's gross profits were $400,000 in 2008 and $540,000 in 2009. Apart from its cost of goods sold, Extreme Edge's operating expenses consist of **selling and administrative expenses** (sometimes called **selling, general, and administrative,** or **SG&A, expenses)**. Deducting these recurring expenses from gross profit determines income from continuing operations. This income number represents earnings from core business activities.[10] Our Internet merchant made income from continuing operations of $55,000 from selling merchandise in its second year of business (2009).

Other revenues (and gains) and expenses (and losses) change income, but do not affect operating income. The most prominent item in this category is interest on borrowed funds. Extreme Edge incurred a $20,000 **interest (financial) expense** in 2009, which represented interest on borrowed funds (i.e., notes payable).[11] Adjusting operating income for non-operating expenses (and revenues) produces pretax income. Governments tax these earnings on a percentage basis, producing **income tax expense (provision for income tax)**. Extreme Edge's tax rate was 40% for each year reported, as derived by dividing income tax expense by pretax earnings. In 2008, for example, we compute the income tax rate as follows: $22,000 / $55,000 = 40%.

STATEMENT OF SHAREHOLDERS' EQUITY

There are two primary components of the statement of shareholders' equity: contributed capital and retained earnings. This statement reports the beginning and ending amounts, as well as the changes. Let us examine both aspects of shareholders' equity in detail.

As we discussed earlier in this chapter, contributed capital reports the owners' investment in a business. Equity investors transfer resources from their personal lives for shares of corporate ownership.[12] Two stock classes exist: Corporations issue **common stock**, and in some instances, **preferred stock**. This latter ownership category is a more conservative form of investment than common stock. Preferred shareholders receive dividends before common shareholders do, but their return on investment (in the form of dividends) is usually lower than that for common stockholders.[13]

The selling price of the stock (fair value or market value) differs from its **par value** (or **legal capital**).[14] Firms identify the amount paid above par value, and report it as **additional paid in capital (paid in capital in excess of par)**. The amount of stock at its par value plus the amount of additional paid in capital equals total contributed capital. Extreme Edge sold common stock worth $420,000 in 2008, and an additional $80,000 the next year. We compute an average selling price of $10 per share in 2008 because $420,000 of contributed capital divided by 42,000 shares equals $10 per share.[15] Similarly, common stock has a par value of $1 per share ($42,000 / 42,000 shares).

Retained earnings are the cumulative amount of income kept within the business for all the years the business has operated. Managers need to remember that retained earnings are intangible: this concept does not have physical substance! Inasmuch as revenues and expenses do not equal cash inflows and outflows, net income does not equal net cash. Consequently, retained earnings summarizes the conceptual total of income kept within the business, and does not equal cash reported on the balance sheet. Extreme Edge did not have any earnings when it started business on January 1, 2008. It earned $33,000 in income its first year but declared and paid dividends of $8,000.[16] Thus, the company retained earnings of $25,000 in 2008. That amount, in turn, became the 2009 beginning balance of retained earnings. Undistributed income of $19,000 in Extreme Edge's second business year increased retained earnings to $44,000 by December 31, 2009.

BALANCE SHEET

The balance sheet, or statement of financial position, reports resources and claims against those resources at the end of each reporting period. Assets, liabilities, and shareholders' equity are the more prevalent business terms than the more economically oriented phrases *resources* and *claims to them*. We now investigate how Extreme Edge discloses each of these three balance sheet elements.

Assets are revenue-producing resources. More specifically, entities report future economic benefits, which they control as the result of past transactions. They classify assets as either current or long-term resources, based on their convertibility into cash. Extreme Edge, like all companies, converts **current assets** into cash within one year or one operating cycle, whichever is longer.[17] Long-term assets produce cash indirectly. These means of production (plant and equipment) generate revenues, which, in turn, yield cash. **Noncurrent assets** exist for more than one reporting period; hence, their long-term designation and distinction from current assets on the balance sheet. The three major categories of long-term assets are financial investments; property, plant, and equipment; and intangible assets.

Liquidity, or a resource's nearness to cash, determines the sequence of current asset disclosures. *Cash* appears as the first current asset because it is readily available to pay the maturing obligations (liabilities) of the firm.[18] A company next discloses its *short-term investments*. These debt and equity positions in other entities are liquid because management intends to sell them in the financial markets in the near term.[19] *Accounts receivable* represent expected collections of unpaid customers' bills. *Inventory* reports the historical cost of unsold products at the end of the reporting period.[20] *Prepaid expenses* represent advanced payment made for future expenses such as insurance, rent, and advertising. Unlike other current assets, firms do not convert these accounts into cash; however, the reporting entity consumes them in the normal course of operating a business. (Prepaid expenses are usually immaterial in amount.)

Extreme Edge reported $45,000 of unencumbered cash and no short-term investments by the end of its second year of business. The company had $140,000 of net accounts receivable at that time. Aggregate (or gross) receivables exceeded that amount, but an *allowance* was made for estimated customer defaults (i.e., not everyone pays their bills). The company owned $250,000 of merchandise at year-end that it expected to sell at marked-up prices. Extreme Edge also had $5,000 worth of prepaid expenses (such as rent paid in advance) at the end of 2009.

Property, plant, and equipment represent a firm's productive, long-term tangible resources. A reporting entity charges the historical cost of these assets against revenues (as depreciation expense) over their productive (revenue-producing) lives. The accumulation of this cost allocation reduces the amount of an asset on the balance sheet to its **book value (carrying** or **net value).** Our hypothetical retailer discloses $400,000 and $380,000 of net equipment at the end of 2008 and 2009, respectively. Managers examine financial statement interrelationships to deduce these ending balances. For instance, Extreme Edge purchased $500,000 of fixed assets in 2008, according to its cash flows statement. That statement also disclosed depreciation expense of $100,000. The 2008 book value of property, plant, and equipment, therefore, is $400,000 ($500,000 cost - $100,000 accumulated depreciation).

Companies usually report **long-term financial investments** prior to property, plant, and equipment disclosures on the balance sheet. Management acquires debt and equity securities of other entities and does not intend to sell them within the next year in such cases. Extreme Edge did not have any such investments; consequently, it did not report that asset category on its balance sheets. (The Internet company's lack of financial investments is not surprising because Extreme Edge, like most new companies, used all of its available capital for business operations.)

Intangible assets mirror property, plant, and equipment, except for their lack of physical substance. A company controls a right, often a legal one, to do something with its intangible assets. Those non-tangible rights help generate revenues. Patents, copyrights, franchises, leaseholds, trademarks, and trade names exemplify intangible assets. In Extreme Edge's case, the company acquired a proprietary customer database at a cost of $25,000. The company has amortized (similar to the depreciation of property, plant, and equipment) these lists of potential customers during a five-year period at $5,000 per year.[21] Consequently, Extreme Edge reports a $20,000 intangible asset at the end of 2008.

Liabilities are future economic sacrifices arising from present obligations to transfer assets or provide services that arose from past transactions. Balance sheets categorize them as either current (short-term) or noncurrent (long-term) liabilities, depending on payment date.

Current liabilities, such as obligations to vendors, employees, property owners, advertisers, utility companies, and taxing authorities, require cash payment within the next year. Unlike current assets, which companies list in order of liquidity, current liabilities follow no strict disclosure patterns. Extreme Edge reported $71,000 worth of current liabilities at the end of its second year of business. Its *accounts payable* represents vendors' obligations for previously purchased inventory.[22] The firm's *accrued liabilities* are the sum of the unpaid bills for other operating costs.

Existing obligations payable beyond the next reporting period define **long-term (noncurrent) liabilities**. Long-term obligations include bonds payable, notes payable, and mortgages payable. Companies pay some debts periodically over many years, such as mortgages on property; therefore, they partition the debt into current and long-term components. In our case, Extreme Edge owed money to its bank on two notes. The company borrowed $120,000 in 2008 and $100,000 in the following year, but it will not pay either obligation in 2009 or 2010; hence, they disclose both notes as long-term liabilities.

Ownership claims to the assets of the firm equal shareholders' equity. Balance sheets disclose contributed capital and retained earnings, which firms initially disclose in their statements of shareholders' equity. Notice that common stock, additional paid in capital, and retained earnings on Extreme Edge's 2008 balance sheet equal those account balances on its statement of shareholders' equity at the end of that year. This relationship among equity disclosures is another example of how financial statements interrelate, or articulate.

STATEMENT OF CASH FLOWS

The statement of cash flows differs from the other three financial statements in that it reports cash information, rather than accrual-based disclosures. As noted earlier, this statement reports three types of cash flows: operating, investing, and financing activities. The latter two sections *directly* report how much cash came into and went out of a business during a reporting period. Operating activities usually disclose cash activities *indirectly* by reconciling net income to operating cash flows.

The most important portion of this statement is the **cash flows from operating activities (CFOs)** section. It reports net cash produced or consumed by the core activity of a business, or its central wealth-building endeavor. The statement reports operating cash flows on either a *direct* or an *indirect* basis. The direct method reports cash received from the sale of goods and services and cash paid to suppliers, employees, creditors (for interest), and taxing authorities. The indirect method reconciles accrual-based net income to operating cash flows by reporting noncash items and changes in current balance sheet accounts. Direct cash flows provide more information to financial statement users, but most companies report on an indirect basis.

Reporting on an indirect basis, Extreme Edge disclosed an operating cash increase of $23,000 in 2008 and a $63,000 decrease in 2009. They added depreciation of equipment and customer database amortization to net income when determining operating cash flows, because those expenses did not require cash payments. Extreme Edge also adjusted income for current account changes (excluding cash) in order to reconcile to cash flows produced by operations.

Note, for example, that the firm subtracted the $20,000 accounts receivable increase in 2009 ($120,000 to $140,000) from net income when computing its 2009 CFOs. They did so because those receivables reflected accrual-based sales revenues, which increased 2009 income, but did not produce cash in 2009. Conversely, the company added its $5,000 decrease in prepaid expenses ($10,000 to $5,000) to its 2009 operating cash flows. That adjustment represents consumption of items purchased with cash during 2008, but expensed in 2009. Expense recognition in 2009 decreased net income, but not cash flow; consequently, Extreme Edge added the account's 2009 net decrease when computing its 2009 cash flows.

The second section of the cash flows statement reports **cash flows from investing activities (CFIs)**. These disclosures inform financial statement users about cash used for the acquisition of fixed assets, and cash generated from their disposal. As a business start-up, Extreme Edge used cash to buy assets. Therefore, it had net cash outflows from investing activities during its first two years of business. The cost of equipment ($500,000) and customer database ($25,000) in 2008, and additional purchase of equipment in 2009 ($100,000), reduced the company's ending cash balances in those years.

The final portion of the cash flow statement reports **cash flows from financing activities (CFFs)**. This section of the statement contains information about cash received from investors and cash returned to them. As such, it measures changes in long-term liabilities and shareholders' equity for a reporting period. The Internet retailer generated cash from financing activities during its first two years of business. These contributions reflect the normal pattern of financing cash flows for a new business as investors inject cash to get the company started. Stock issues accounted for $420,000 and $80,000 of cash in 2008 and 2009, respectively. Long-term bank financing (notes payable) produced cash inflows of $220,000 ($120,000 in 2008 and $100,000 in 2009). Dividend payments, however, reduced these cash infusions by $8,000 and $2,000 in 2008 and 2009, respectively.

FINANCIAL STATEMENT ARTICULATION

Chapter 1 introduced the concept of articulation, which means that the four financial statements work together to provide meaningful information to their readers. We now draw on the 2008 and 2009 Extreme Edge financial statements presented in Exhibit 2-1, and the preceding financial statement discussion to illustrate financial statement articulation directly. (Recall that Extreme Edge began operating on January 1, 2008; therefore, beginning balances for that year are zero.)

We conclude this section of Chapter 2 with Exhibit 2-2. It demonstrates how specific accounts interrelate with one another.

Exhibit 2-2
Financial Statement Articulation (in thousands)
Extreme Edge, Inc.

Cash Reconciliation

Accounts	2009	2008
Beginning cash balance—January 1	$30	$0
+/- net change in cash (per the statement of cash flows)	15	30
Ending cash balance (per the December 31 balance sheet)	$45	$30

Contributed Capital Reconciliation (#1)

Accounts	2009	2008
Beginning contributed capital—January 1	$420	$0
+ Common stock (per the statement of shareholders' equity)	8	42
+ Additional paid in capital (per the statement of shareholders' equity)	72	378
Ending contributed capital (per the December 31 balance sheet)	$500	$420

Contributed Capital Reconciliation (#2)

Accounts	2009	2008
Beginning contributed capital—January 1	$420	$0
+ Issue common stock (per the statement of cash flows)	80	420
Ending contributed capital (per the December 31 balance sheet)	$500	$420

Retained Earnings (#1)

Accounts	2009	2008
Beginning retained earnings—January 1	$25	$0
+ Net income (per the statement of shareholders' equity)	21	33
- Dividends (per the statement of shareholders' equity)	(2)	(8)
Ending retained earnings (per the December 31 balance sheet)	$44	$25

Retained Earnings (#2)

Accounts	2009	2008
Beginning retained earnings—January 1	$25	$0
+ Net income (per the income statement)	21	33
- Dividends (per the statement of cash flows)	(2)	(8)
Ending retained earnings (per the December 31 balance sheet)	$44	$25

Customer Database[23]

Accounts	2009	2008
Purchase of customer database (per the statement of cash flows)	$ 0	$25
Net or book value of database—January 1	20	25
Amortization expense (per the statement of cash flows)	(5)	(5)
Net or book value of database (per the December 31 balance sheet)	$15	$20

Equipment

Accounts	2009	2008
Purchase of equipment (per the statement of cash flows)	$100	$500
Net or book value of equipment—January 1	400	500
Depreciation expense (per the statement of cash flows)	(120)	(100)
Net or book value of equipment (per the December 31 balance sheet)	$380	$400

NOT-FOR-PROFIT ACCOUNTING

Perhaps the greatest disparity in financial statement disclosures arises when entities do not share the same fundamental financial objective. The material presented up to this point assumes the disclosures of a for-profit corporation. Shareowners invest their capital in these types of enterprises with the expectation that the company will provide them with an acceptable return on their investments. Consequently, the entity strives to maximize owners' wealth.[24] The financial statements, the output of the accounting system, report the results of the firm's wealth creating activities in such accounts as net income, dividends, and retained earnings. Corporate accounting also controls management behavior by insuring that the professionals who run the company work for the benefit of the owners.[25] Managers fulfill their fiduciary obligation to the owners by creating wealth for them.

Not all entities, however, seek profits. We now explore how **not-for-profit (NFP) organizations** report financial performance and position.[26] First, we examine the objectives of NFP financial reporting. Next, we discuss accounting for voluntary health and welfare organizations (VHWO). The final section of this chapter presents an overview of governmental reporting.

OBJECTIVES

Not-for-profit entities exist to meet their specifically designated mission. Such a mission involves fulfilling a societal objective rather than maximizing institutional (i.e., owners) wealth. The NFP's accounting system, therefore, helps the organization plan and control operations so that it can meet its societal objective. In order to understand NFP accounting, the reader should bear in mind the following characteristics of a not-for-profit entity.

- Collective ownership—a broad group of people own or control the entity (e.g., the citizens of the United States *own* the federal government; the donors to the American Cancer Society *own* the charity).
- Ownership right—a certain standing (e.g., citizenship or affiliation), rather than a purchased interest (e.g., stock ownership), determines control of the entity.
- Consensus decision-making—all stakeholders share power and consensus (usually a majority vote) determines decisions.
- Need based—NFPs provide goods and services to owners as needed, rather than as purchased (in other words, not-for-profits do not have a market-based pricing mechanism).
- Importance of a budget—not-for profits establish *control* of the owners' resources, to insure *compliance* with laws and regulations regarding those resources, and to hold elected or appointed individuals *accountable* in expending those resources.

ORGANIZATIONS

There are two primary types of not-for-profit entities:

1. Government entities (GE)—cities, counties, school districts, states, and the federal government.
2. Voluntary health and welfare organizations (VHWO)—charities, medical providers, educational institutions, labor unions, political parties, religious organizations, and so forth.

Taken together, people refer to these two groups as **governmental and other not-for-profits (G&NP)**.

Some types of not-for-profits exist as both the governmental and voluntary organizations. For example, a county government or a religious order may control a medical center. Similarly, both states and private organizations operate colleges and universities. The critical distinction from an accounting perspective is the entity's classification as either a government or a voluntary organization. This dichotomy matters because generally accepted accounting principles differ for the two types of entities.

The **Governmental Accounting Standards Board (GASB)** sets standards for state and local governments while the **Financial Accounting Standards Board (FASB)** sets standards for voluntary organizations (as well as for-profit businesses).[27] Consequently, the G&NP must conform to specific accounting standards and disclose the appropriate types of financial statements.[28] The remainder of this chapter examines the primary accounting issues for GEs and VWHOs. We begin by considering the financial disclosures of a voluntary organization.

VOLUNTARY ORGANIZATION ACCOUNTING

Accounting for this not-for-profit segment reflects accounting in the for-profit sector, except that contributions provide initial financing rather than stock sales. **Donations** or **contributions** are voluntary nonreciprocal remittances made to the organization.

Donors sometimes attach contractual covenants to their donations. For example, a contributor may donate funds to a not-for-profit medical center only if the hospital builds a new cancer unit. The accounting system classifies such contractual restrictions to donated resources as **restricted assets**.[29] The NFP, in other words, must use those contributions for their intended purpose. Restricted assets, therefore, are unavailable to meet normal operating costs.

Voluntary health and welfare organizations report three primary financial statements: statement of activities (similar to a for-profit's income statement), balance sheet, and statement of cash flows.[30] We now demonstrate the accounting process for a voluntary organization in a case format.

VOLUNTARY ORGANIZATION CASE

The Redlands Medical Alliance (RMA) is a local charitable organization that provides basic medical services to indigent people in the Inland Empire at little or no cost. In addition, the organization offers free medical education with the aim of preventing illness and other medical problems. RMA started its voluntary health and welfare organization in late 2009 with funding from a prominent local family and began operations in 2010.

The case presents the accounting for the Redlands Medical Alliance in four steps (amounts in millions):

1. Account for initial 2009 financing
2. Record the 2010 journal entries
3. Report the 2010 statement of activities and balance sheet
4. Close the temporary accounts at the end of 2010

2009 Financing

Item	Transactions	Journal Entry
a.	RMA receives a $30 donation at the end of 2009.	Cash—R 30 Contributions—R* 30

* where R equals restricted and U equals unrestricted

2009 Closing Entry

Item	Transactions	Journal Entry
b.	Close the contribution to net assets.	Contributions—R 30 Net assets—R 30

Redlands Medical Alliance
2009 Statement of Activities (in millions)

Change in Unrestricted Net Assets $ 0
Change in Restricted Net Assets—Contributions   <u>30</u>
   Change in Net Assets   **$30**

Redlands Medical Alliance
Balance Sheet
At December 31, 2009 (in millions)

Unrestricted Assets	$ 0	Liabilities	$0
Restricted Assets:			
Cash	30	Net Assets:	
Total Restricted Assets	<u>30</u>	Unrestricted	0
		Restricted	<u>30</u>
Total Assets	**$30**	**Total Liabilities and Net Assets**	**$30**

2010 Operating Events

Item	Transaction	Journal Entry

c.	RMA receives unrestricted pledges of $50. It does not expect to collect $4 of the pledges.	Pledges receivable—U 50
		    Allowance for uncollectible pledges 4
		    Contributions—U 46

d.	Collects $38 in pledges	Cash—U 38 Pledges receivable—U 38
e.	Pays $35 for operating expenses	Operating expenses—U 35 Cash—U 35
f.	Collects $7 for medical services performed	Cash—U 7 Service revenues—U 7
g.	Accrues operating expenses of $9	Operating expenses—U 9 Accounts payable—U 9

Redlands Medical Alliance
2010 Statement of Activities (in millions)

Change in Unrestricted Net Assets:

Contributions	$46
Service revenues	7
Less: operating expenses	<u>44</u>
Net change in unrestricted net assets	9

Change in Restricted Net Assets:

Contributions	<u>0</u>
Change in Net Assets	**$ 9**

Redlands Medical Alliance
Balance Sheet
At December 31, 2010 (in millions)

Unrestricted Assets		Liabilities	
Cash	$10	Accounts payable	$9
Pledges receivable	12		
Less: allowance for uncoll.	<u>(4)</u>		
Unrestricted net assets	18		
Restricted Assets		Net Assets	
Cash	<u>30</u>	Unrestricted	9
		Restricted	<u>30</u>
Total Assets	**$48**	**Total Liabilities and Net Assets**	**$48**

2010 Closing Entries

Item	Transaction	Journal Entry		
h.	Close unrestricted revenues and contributions	Contributions—U	46	
		Service Revenues—U	7	
		Unrestricted net assets		53
i.	Close expenses	Unrestricted net assets	44	
		Operating expenses		44

GOVERNMENTAL ACCOUNTING

Governmental accounting differs from the accounting for voluntary NFPs, due to its focus on **fund accounting**. A **fund** is a separate financial and accounting entity within a government organization designed to meet the regulatory and administrative requirements of the organization. For example, the city of Redlands (the reporting entity) has numerous funds (accounting entities) to account for the activities of the city as a whole. This concept contrasts to the economic entity assumption that applies to for-profit businesses and voluntary NFP organizations.

Governments classify funds into two broad categories.[31] They are as follows:

1. **Governmental (expendable) funds**—account for general government and government-related services (e.g., public safety, parks and recreation, and so forth).
2. **Proprietary (nonexpendable) funds**—provide services for fees and are run similar to a for-profit business (e.g., a city providing water to its residents, a country selling electricity to its citizens).

Proprietary fund accounting is similar to that for a profit-seeking business. Moreover, the financial reporting requirements for such nonexpendable funds virtually mirror those for VHWO financial reporting. Consequently, our current discussion will focus on governmental, or expendable, fund accounting.

GOVERNMENTAL FUNDS

The most prominent governmental (expendable) funds are the following ones:

- General Fund—the primary governmental fund that accounts for the majority operating activities of the entity (e.g., public safety, street maintenance, etc.)
- Special Revenue Funds—a limited-life fund that monitors resources dedicated for a special purpose (e.g., an additional sales tax used to fund a municipal sports stadium)
- Capital Project Funds—a multi-year fund that controls capital improvements (e.g., the construction of a school, public library, or fire station)
- Debt Service Funds—a fund that controls repayment on long-term borrowed funds (often used in conjunction with a capital project fund)

The critical feature in understanding fund accounting is that the fund's balance sheet consists of only current assets and liabilities. The accounting equation for a governmental fund is as follows:

$$\text{Current assets} = \text{current liabilities} + \text{fund balance}$$
$$\text{or}$$
$$\text{Current assets} - \text{current liabilities} = \text{fund balance}$$

In addition to the governmental (expendable) funds stated above, a related set of accounts must exist for the government in its entirety. Accountants call these the non-fund accounts.[32] The **non-fund accounts** report a government's long-term assets and long-term liabilities. The non-fund accounts' balance sheet equation is as follows:

$$\text{General capital assets} = \text{general long-term liabilities} + \text{net assets}$$

Recall that a specific governmental fund, such as the general fund, only contains current accounts (assets and liabilities). The entity as a whole, however, needs its non-fund accounts to control its long-term assets and liabilities. Think of it this way: the general fund uses the resources generated by tax revenues to meet public safety obligations; consequently, taxes receivable are part of the general governmental fund's balance sheet. The general fund, however, does not (and cannot) own the police and fire stations. The municipality or county owns the public safety buildings.[33] The governmental entity, therefore, reports those facilities in its non-fund accounts.

BUDGETING OF GOVERNMENTAL FUNDS

The budgeting process for a general government fund is one in which the appropriate executive authority (e.g., the governor) determines a budget, and an approving authority (e.g., state legislature) approves it, or a modified version of it. Law fixes governmental fund budgets. This means that the fund cannot expend more than the budgeted resources without expressed legislative authority. Authorized budgeted expenditures define **appropriations**.

Budgeted revenues will provide the resources necessary to settle the obligations arising from fund expenditures. Taxation provides the primary source of fund revenues. The two most prominent types of tax financing at the local level are property tax and sales tax revenues. States derive most of their operating capital from personal and corporate income taxes, as well as sales taxes. Regardless of source, taxes are involuntary, non-exchange types of transaction. These terms apply because citizens involuntarily pay taxes, and they do not necessarily receive goods and services in proportion to the taxes paid.[34]

The accounting system formally enters the budget into the fund accounting system. Assume that the city of Redlands approved a general fund budget that expected to collect $10 million in tax revenues ($8 million from property taxes and $2 million from sales taxes) and anticipated making $9 million of general fund expenditures. The budget entries (in millions) are as follows:

Date[35]	Accounts	Debit	Credit
1/1/10	Estimated revenues—property taxes	8	
	Estimated revenues—sales taxes	2	
	Unreserved fund balance		10
1/1/10	Unreserved fund balance	9	
	Appropriations		9

The reader should note that the budgetary entries apparently invert revenue and appropriation accounts (e.g., debiting revenues instead of crediting them). This is *not* a mistake. The accounting system records budgetary entries this way in order to reflect economic reality. Note that the net unreserved fund balance will increase by a $1 million if Redlands meets it budget.[36] The city anticipates that its revenues will produce $10 million in current assets and its expenditures will consume $9 million of those resources if all goes according to plan. Consequently, the fund's unreserved balance sheet will be as follows:

$1 million current assets = $0 current liabilities + $1 million fund balance.

The subsequent closing of accounts will adjust net current assets and the corresponding fund balance if actual results differ from budgeted expectations.

EXPENDITURES AND ENCUMBRANCES

You may have noticed a slight discrepancy in the preceding discussion in the wording related to the concept of economic sacrifice for a governmental fund. We used the term expenditure in the preceding section rather than *expense*. Recall from the earlier chapters that an expense is a cost (or portion of a cost) that the firm matches to revenues in a specific accounting period.

Expenditures and expenses are similar concepts, but they are not identical. While both relate to a theoretical notion of economic sacrifice, expenditures are broader in scope than expenses. A fund's **expenditures** equal the amount of financial resources used during a reporting period for current operations, *capital outlays*, and *debt service*. Expenditures are, in other words, the *total* cost of goods delivered and services rendered by a governmental fund in a reporting period. Capital outlays represent the cost of acquiring assets, and debt service reflects the settlement of long-term liabilities. Consequently, the fund's income statement subtracts capital costs and debt service, as well as operating expense in determining income.[37] Unlike fund accounting, for-profit firms do not subtract these items from revenues in their current reporting period.

Transactions sometimes affect both a fund and the non-fund accounts. For example, assume that Redlands expended $100,000 from its general fund for a new fire truck. The city would record $100,000 in general fund expenditures when it incurs those costs. Those expenditures would reduce net current assets on the general fund's balance sheet. In addition, the non-fund accounts would reflect a $100,000 increase in capital (long-term) assets for their cost. Net assets in the non-fund accounts would increase by $100,000 in order to maintain the integrity of the non-fund accounts.[38] We summarize the effect of the capital assets as follows:

General fund: current assets (-$100,000) = current liabilities $0 + fund balance (-$100,000)
Non-fund accounts: capital assets (+$100,000) = long-term liabilities $0 + net assets (+$100,000)

As noted, a fund's budgeted appropriations represent the legally approved amount of total expenditures. The fund pays for (or incurs an obligation to pay for) many goods and services when it receives such goods and services. In these instances, the government fund expends a portion of the fund's appropriation. Oftentimes, the fund knows with virtually certainty that *future* expenditures will consume a portion of its appropriations. A fund accounting system creates a mechanism for many of its anticipated expenditures. **Encumbrances** are a claim against appropriations for future expenditures.

Consider the Redlands budget (stated above) to grasp the concept of an encumbrance. Assume that the city is contractually obligated to pay salaries totaling $4 million from its general fund. That $4 million constitutes an encumbrance against appropriations. Such encumbrances are *expenditures in process*; they will become expenditures with the passage of time (as city employees earn their salaries during the reporting period). Viewed another way, the fund can only purchase $5 million of other goods and services (i.e., $9 million appropriation - $4 million salary encumbrance).

Two encumbrance-related issues can arise. First, a fund records the exact cost of encumbered goods and services as expenditures when it receives them.

The encumbered amount may differ from the expended sum. Assume for the moment that the Redlands' general fund salaries encumbered for $4 million actually amounted to $5 million. Unexpected overtime created the unfavorable variance. The city reports an expenditure of $5 million and cancels its $4 million encumbrance. The closing process reconciles the $1 million difference. The second issue is that a fund may encumber a portion of the appropriation toward the end of one reporting period and recognize the expenditure in the next one. The outstanding encumbrance represents a claim on a portion of the fund's balance in such instances.

FUND ACCOUNTING

The remainder of this section illustrates fund accounting by extending the Redlands general fund budget example (all amounts in millions).[39] We assume that during 2010 Redlands:

- Collected $8 in property tax revenues and billed another $1 that it has yet to collect
- Collected $2 in sales tax
- Paid $3 for operations
- Encumbered $4 for salaries
- Paid $5 for salaries
- Encumbered (but did not pay) $2 toward the end of the year for operations

General Fund Entries

Accounts	Debit	Credit
Cash	8	
Property tax receivable	1	
Property tax revenues		9
Cash	2	
Sales tax revenues		2
Operating expenditures	3	
Cash		3

Encumbrance for salaries	4	
Reserve for encumbrance—salaries		4
Salary expenditure	5	
Cash		5
Reserve for encumbrance	4	
Encumbrance for salaries		4
Encumbrance for operations	2	
Reserve for encumbrance—operations		2

As a result of the above transactions, Redlands would report the following financial statements.[40]

Redlands General Fund
2010 Statement of Revenues and Expenditures (in millions)

Revenues:		
Property taxes	$9	
Sales taxes	2	11
Expenditures:		
Operating expenditures	3	
Salaries expenditures	5	8
Excess of revenues over expenditures (surplus)		**$3**

Redlands General Fund
December 31, 2010 Balance Sheet (in millions)

Cash	$2	
Property taxes receivable	1	
Total current assets		**$3**
Total current liabilities		$0
Fund Balance:		
Unreserved fund balance	1	
Reserve for encumbrances—operations	2	
Total fund balance		3
Total liabilities and fund balance		**$3**

The reader should note that a fund's statement of revenues and expenditures is analogous to a for-profit's income statement. Financial statement users generally refer to the excess of revenues over expenditures as a **surplus**. A **deficit** results when fund expenditures exceed revenues.

Redlands would also make the following closing entries to assure the integrity of its general fund accounts:

General Fund Closing Entries

Date	Accounts	Debit	Credit
12/31/10	Property tax revenues	9	
	Sales tax revenues	2	
	Est. revenues—property taxes		8
	Est. revenues—sales taxes		2
	Unreserved fund balance		1
	Appropriations	9	
	Unreserved fund balance	1	
	Operating expenditures		3
	Salaries expenditures		5
	Encumbrance—operations		2

The closing process results in a $1 million *unreserved* fund balance (i.e., $1 million from the budget + $1 million from closing revenues - $1 million from closing expenditures). The $2 million *reserved* fund balance for encumbrances reported on the balance sheet exists because the accounting process does *not* close the $2 million *reserve for encumbrance* account. (It only closes the encumbrance account.)

Summary

Chapter 2 examined detailed accounting disclosures. The first section of the chapter discussed the composition of each of the four financial statements. It defined critical accounts and presented how organizations disclosed them. After establishing the financial statement composition, Chapter 2 illustrated the concept of financial statement articulation. Numerous examples based on the Extreme Edge set of financials illustrated how statement data interrelate. For example, the reader learned how the income statement, statement of shareholders' equity, and statement of cash flows all provide data that appears on the balance sheet.

The second half of Chapter 2 addressed the accounting processes for not-for-profit organizations. It examined the accounting for both voluntary health and welfare organizations as well as governmental entities. Students learned that financial statement nomenclature changed, due to the non-profit orientation of such firms. The final section of the chapter addressed concept of fund accounting, which is unique to governmental entities.

Key Terms

Additional paid in capital (paid in capital in excess of par)
Appropriation
Book value (carrying value or net value)
Cash flows from operating activities
Cash flows from financing activities
Cash flows from investing activities
Common stock
Contributed capital
Cost of goods sold (cost of sales)
Current assets
Current liabilities
Deficit
Dividends
Donations or contributions
Earnings per share (EPS)
Encumbrance
Expenditures
Fund accounting
Gains
Governmental (expendable) funds
Governmental Accounting Standards Board (GASB)
Governmental and other not-for-profits (G&NP)
Gross profit (gross margin, gross profit margin)
Income tax expense (provision for income tax)
Intangible assets
Interest (financial) expense
Liquidity
Long-term (noncurrent) liabilities
Long-term financial investments
Losses
Multiple-step income statement
Noncurrent assets
Non-fund accounts
Not-for-profit (NFP) organizations
Par value (or legal capital)
Preferred stock
Property, plant, and equipment
Proprietary (nonexpendable) funds

Restricted assets
Retained earnings
Selling and administrative expenses (selling, general and administrative;
SG&A expenses)
Single-step income statement
Surplus

Assignments

Accounting Concepts Crossword

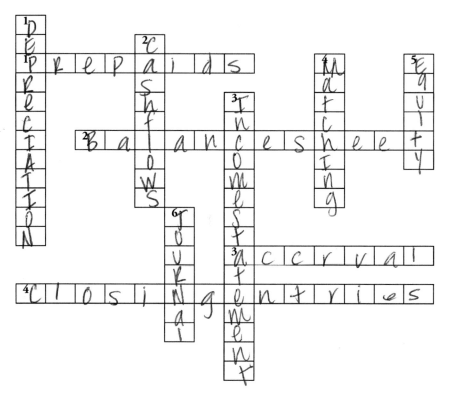

Across

[1] Costs such as rent, interest, insurance, etc., that are paid in advance of actually incurring them.

[2] Financial statements that display a company's financial position at a single point in time.

[3] Method of accounting whereby revenues are recognized when earned and expenses are recognized in the period incurred, regardless of the exchange of cash.

[4] Entries that reduce the balance of nominal (temporary) accounts to zero.

Down

[1] Spreading the cost of an asset over several periods.

[2] Financial statement that displays a company's sources and uses of cash over a period of time.

[3] Financial statements that display a company's revenues and expenses over a period of time.

[4] Principle that dictates expenses should be matched with revenues, whenever possible.

[5] Represents the owners' claims against a company's resources.

[6] The book of original entry. A chronological listing of transactions expressed in terms of debits and credits.

Discussion Items

What Would Your Accountant Say?

A meeting of company executives has been called to go over the annual financial report, which includes the balance sheet, income statement, statement of stockholders' equity, and statement of cash flows. The new VP of Marketing, who has little accounting knowledge, asks you to describe the purpose of each financial statement and their interrelationships. What would your accountant say to the executives?

Theory vs. Practice

As pointed out in the chapter reading materials, governments are required by law to develop, adopt, and operate under an annual balanced budget. Many governmental budgets are not always designed to allocate scarce resources for the best economic uses. They also may have a political basis wherein budget battles are fought over contending interests, ideologies, programs, and agencies.

In theory, most for-profit entities could benefit from a formal budgeting process such as is required for governments; however, in practice many companies do not implement such procedures. Discuss the pros and cons of implementing a formal budgeting process, and if possible, give real world examples of budgeting successes and failures from your own past work experience.

Problems

Problem 2-1

Use the Extreme Edge financial statement information from Exhibit 2-1 to complete the following financial statement articulation tables for 2010 and 2011.

Cash Reconciliation

Accounts	2011	2010
Beginning cash balance—January 1	187	45
+/- net change in cash (per the statement of cash flows)	(153)	142
Ending cash balance (per the December 31 balance sheet)	34	187

Contributed Capital Reconciliation (#1)

Accounts	2011	2010
Beginning contributed capital—January 1	500	500
+ Common stock (per the statement of shareholders' equity)	—	—
+ Additional paid in capital (per the statement of shareholders' equity)	—	—
Ending contributed capital (per the December 31 balance sheet)	500	500

Contributed Capital Reconciliation (#2)

Accounts	2011	2010
Beginning contributed capital—January 1		
+ Issue common stock (per the statement of cash flows)		
Ending contributed capital (per the December 31 balance sheet)		

Retained Earnings (#1)

Accounts	2011	2010
Beginning retained earnings—January 1	65	44
+ Net income (per the statement of shareholders' equity)	(9)	22
- Dividends (per the statement of shareholders' equity)	—	(2)
Ending retained earnings (per the December 31 balance sheet)	56	65

Retained Earnings (#2)

Accounts	2011	2010
Beginning retained earnings—January 1		
+ Net income (per the income statement)		
- Dividends (per the statement of cash flows)		
Ending retained earnings (per the December 31 balance sheet)		

Customer Database[41]

Accounts	2011	2010
Purchase of customer database (per the statement of cash flows)		
Net or book value of database—January 1		

Amortization expense (per the statement of cash flows)		
Net or book value of database (per the December 31 balance sheet)		

Equipment

Accounts	2011	2010
Purchase of equipment (per the statement of cash flows)		
Net or book value of equipment—January 1		
Depreciation expense (per the statement of cash flows)		
Net or book value of equipment (per the December 31 balance sheet)		

Problem 2-2

Use the Redlands General Fund 2010 statement of revenues and expenditures and balance sheet from this chapter as the starting point for this problem. Redlands had the following 2011 transactions (in millions):

    a. Budgeted $9 for property tax revenues and $2 for sales tax revenues
    b. Budgeted $11 for expenditures
    c. Billed property owners $9 for taxes
    d. Encumbered $5 for salaries
    e. Paid $1 for operations that it had encumbered for $2 in 2010
    f. Received $10 in property tax payments
    g. Accrued the $2 of sales tax revenues
    h. Paid $6 for non-encumbered 2011 operating expenditures
    i. Paid $5 for encumbered salaries (encumbered in item d)

Required:

    1. Record the journal entries.
    2. Report the 2011 statement of revenues and expenditures and the balance sheet for the general fund.
    3. Close the general fund accounts.

Case 2-1

You led a group of investors in purchasing Zodiak, Inc. from its founder and namesake at the beginning of 2004. You financed the $40 million acquisition of this manufacturer of quality industrial components with equal amounts of equity and debt capital. Your investment team provided the majority of owner financing, and other investors purchased stock to supplement your group's equity infusion. A $20 million, 6% loan from First National Bank financed the remainder of the purchase.

You resigned as chief executive officer (CEO) after the firm's fourth fiscal year, which ended on December 31, 2007, in order to pursue other business opportunities. You continued in your capacity as chair of Zodiak's Board of Directors (BOD). The BOD elected Johannes Skilling as CEO, effective January 1, 2008, over your objections. Mr. Skilling had a proven record of accomplishment as an executive and demonstrated strong interpersonal skill during the search process; yet, you had an uneasy feeling about him. Specifically, you felt that Skilling took too many unnecessary risks and pushed the envelope too far with overly aggressive financial reporting practices. Although Mr. Skilling was thoroughly vetted, you had "off the record" conversations with trusted business colleagues who echoed your concerns. None was willing, however, to speak on the record. In the end, you acquiesced to the unanimous wish of the rest of the board and ratified the hiring of Mr. Skilling as CEO effective January 1, 2008.

Financial Statements

Zodiak's financial performance during your tenure as CEO was solid, if not spectacular. Corporate profitability ostensibly soared under Skilling's tutelage in 2008. The accompanying spreadsheet contains the annual income statements and statements of cash flow for the last three fiscal years, as well as the last two period's balance sheets. The financial data clearly evidence the superior results Zodiak achieved in 2008, which was the first year that Skilling served as CEO.

Income Statements (in thousands)	3		
For the Years Ended December 31	2008	2007	2006
Sales revenues	$35,735	$31,906	$30,100
Cost of goods sold	13,579	13,608	12,840
Gross profit	22,156	18,298	17,260
Selling, general, and administrative expenses	8,270	8,427	8,025
Depreciation expense	645	640	625
Research and development expense	660	756	700
Operating income	12,581	8,475	7,910
Interest expense	2,000	1,200	1,200
Income before taxes	10,581	7,275	6,710
Income tax expense	4,444	3,056	2,818

Net income	$6,137	$4,219	$3,892

Balance Sheets (in thousands)		
December 31	2008	2007
Assets		
Cash	$5,728	$2,123
Accounts receivable	7,047	6,282
Inventory	5,812	4,531
Other current assets	1,649	134
Current assets	20,236	13,070
Net property, plant, and equipment	33,067	34,737
Total assets	**$53,303**	**$47,807**
Liabilities		
Accounts payable	$4,253	$3,402
Accrued liabilities	889	846
Current liabilities	5,142	4,248
Notes payable	30,000	20,000
Total liabilities	35,142	24,248
Shareholders' Equity		
Common stock	10,000	20,000
Retained earnings	8,161	3,559
Total shareholders' equity	18,161	23,559
Total liabilities and shareholders' equity	**$53,303**	**$47,807**

Statements of Cash Flows (in thousands)			
For the Years Ended December 31	2008	2007	2006
Net income	$6,137	$4,219	$3,892
Depreciation expense	645	640	625
Changes in current assets and current liabilities	(2,667)	193	204
Cash flows from operating activities	4,115	5,052	4,721
Purchase of property, plant, and equipment	(2,275)	(3,400)	(3,250)

Sale of property, plant, and equipment	3,300	---	---
Cash flows from investing activities	1,025	(3,400)	(3,250)
Issuance of debt	10,000	---	---
Purchase of common stock (treasury stock)	(10,000)	---	---
Payment of dividends	(1,535)	(633)	(584)
Cash flows from financing activities	(1,535)	(633)	(584)
Net change in cash	**$3,605**	**$1,019**	**$887**

The 2008 financial results presented in the spreadsheet, however, are unaudited as of this date. (The previous years' financial statements received unqualified or "clean" audit opinions from Zodiak's external accounting firm.)

Reporting Issues

One of your most trusted members of the executive team during your time as CEO was Meg Walters, the corporate controller. In early 2009, Ms. Walters expressed concern to you about a number of accounting issues. In sum, she and her internal audit staff felt that Zodiak's financial reporting was too aggressive, and the firm overstated its 2008 operating performance and year-end financial position. Meg told you that she repeatedly expressed her concerns to Mr. Skilling. He assured her that Zodiak's accounting complied with generally accepted accounting principles (GAAP). At one point, Skilling stated to her, "Our financial statements conform to GAAP. Our managerial judgments about the numbers may be more optimistic than those of the previous administration, but let me assure you that they are legitimate. Moreover, they will pass muster with our new external auditors. I have used the audit firm of Arturo Andersen at my other firms and they have always given me a clean audit opinion. I expect that they will do the same for Zodiak."

Three areas particularly concern Ms. Walters:

- The company booked revenues of approximately $2 million when it shipped product to some of its regular customers at the end of 2008. Zodiak reported these sales even though the customers had not ordered the goods. Skilling stated that the sales would "help" the 2008 numbers. In addition, Zodiak's sales force told the recipients that they could return the goods in 2009 if they did not want them. The firm made no provision for any returns of these sales.

Ms. Walters firmly believed that the customers would return the $2 million of goods in 2009. She knows that Zodiak could sell the goods to other customers when the customers return them. She further notes that Zodiak's cost of goods sold have traditionally been 42.65% of sales revenues.

- The firm reduced cost of goods sold by $1.6 million in 2008 because of "unacceptable raw materials received from vendors during the year." Historically, Zodiak receives about $100,000 of substandard raw materials annually. Per industry standard, the company informs its vendors of defective product. The vendors credit Zodiak's account upon notification. The industrial component manufacturer then reduces its accounts payable and eliminates the inventory from its accounts.
  Mr. Skilling informed Ms. Walters that Zodiak received the majority of unacceptable goods, totaling $1.5 million, in the fourth fiscal quarter. Furthermore, the company has yet to inform its suppliers of this dubious claim. Mr. Skilling expressed no doubt that Zodiak would receive credit from its suppliers for the substandard goods. In anticipation of vendor concurrence, Zodiak reduced its accounts payable by $1.6 million.

- Zodiak added the $1 million cost of corporate reorganization to the balance of its property, plant, and equipment account. Mr. Skilling opined that the restructuring would benefit the firm for at least the next ten years. "And besides," he said, "we recognized 10% of that restructuring cost as a depreciation expense in 2008."

Ms. Walters also states that if Zodiak were to adjust its income statement, then the firm would have to alter its income tax expense. She notes that the firm paid taxing authorizes the full amount of income tax expense for 2008 at the end of that year. She states, "If we did overstate our pretax income, then we would be entitled to a tax refund to the extent that we overpaid the government."

You are very concerned about the issues that Ms. Walters presented to you. You would like to bring them to the full board's attention. In order to do so, you charge Ms. Walters with two tasks:

Required:

1. Recast Zodiak's 2008 income statement and balance sheet to conform to generally accepted accounting principles. (You do *not* have to recast the firm's 2008 statement of cash flows.)

2. Compose an executive summary addressing the issues in your calculations and comment on the firm's 2008 financial performance and its financial position as of December 31, 2008.

Endnotes

1   Synonyms for shareholders' equity include stockholders' equity, owners' equity, and share-owners' equity.

2   The distribution of profits assumes sufficient cash exists to make dividend payments.

3   People commonly refer to this subset of the statement of shareholders' equity as the statement of retained earnings.

4   Such an event is highly unlikely for a start-up company. We discuss these *treasury stock* transactions in the capital structure chapters of the text.

5   The book presents disclosures in reverse chronology, which is the common method of disclosure. In addition, this text adheres to the convention of reporting the two most recent balance sheets but disclosing the last three income statements, statements of shareholders' equity, and statements of cash flows. While some companies report their balance sheets first, we elect to disclose the income statements initially to demonstrate how business operations affect financial position.

6   For a more complete discussion of all of the financial statement elements, refer to the FASB's *Statement of Financial Accounting Concepts No. 6,* "Elements of Financial Statements," (Stamford CT: FASB, 1985).

7   The first three expenses are costs of *operating* Extreme Edge. Interest (financial) expense is Extreme Edge's annual cost of *financing* a portion of its assets through debt.

8   Net income is measured in accordance with generally accepted accounting principles. Other non-GAAP systems exist, such as inflation-adjusted profit levels.

9   These calculations assume the company issued the stock at the beginning of each year.

10 Depreciation expense, salaries expense, utilities expense, and rent expense exemplify operating expenses. Most companies collapse these different types of expenses into just a few line items for disclosure purposes.

11   We assume that the borrowing took place at the beginning of each year. Interest rates were 8.33% in 2008 and 10% in 2009.

12   Cash is the primary means of financing an entity, but investors can exchange other consideration (noncash assets) for stock.

13   Preferred stock features reflect some of the characteristics of long-term debt, rather than equity capital.

14   Par value equals the minimum legal selling price for stock in most states.

15   We could use the same approach for the 2009 stock issue, which generated $80,000 in cash.

16   Cash dividends are the most prevalent form of investor compensation, but not the only kind. Other types, such as stock and property (noncash asset) distributions, exist. In addition, a company needs only to have retained earnings to *declare* a dividend, but it must have the cash (stock or property) to *pay* them. There is a time lag between the declaration date and payment date.

17   An operating cycle is the length of time it takes a company to convert inventory into cash in the ordinary course of business. For most industries, the operating cycle is shorter than one year; consequently, this text assumes current asset conversion within one year.

18   GAAP requires disclosure of restricted cash because it affects liquidity. Moreover, cash dedicated to a long-term use, such as the retirement of a noncurrent note payable, is reported as a long-term investment. Disclosures about cash or reclassifying it as another asset, illustrate the reporting concept of *substance over form*. A company reports the economic substance of its accounts, rather than their legal basis. In this case, companies classify cash as such only if it is unencumbered.

19   Firms sometimes refer to short-term investments as *marketable securities*. Cash conversion is not an issue for short-term investments, because available buyers exist at market-determined prices at all times.

20   Balance sheets technically report inventory at cost or market, whichever is lower. Market value adjustments exceed the scope of this text.

21 Firms amortize intangible assets if they diminish in value over time, but they do not amortize those with a perpetual life.

22 This book defines accounts payable as obligations to suppliers of finished goods or raw materials—products that will be sold to its customers. A broader definition considers all obligations to suppliers of goods and services, regardless of whether buyers purchase for resale purposes, as accounts payable. This definition of accounts payable complicates analysis. Therefore, we classify all non-inventory related short-term obligations as accrued liabilities.

23 Assumes Extreme Edge purchased both the customer database and the equipment at the beginning of the year and apportioned their costs equally over a five-year period.

24 This statement assumes that the corporation acts legally and ethically in maximizing shareowner wealth. Substantial research demonstrates that entities failing to do so cannot maximize long-term profits.

25 While managers may own an equity stake in the firm, individuals who own the great majority of stock are not directly involved in operating the firm.

26 The authors favor the term not-for-profit over the more common nonprofit, because these organizations often do earn profits. In fact, profitable operations contribute to their financial stability and allow the NFPs to meet their mission better.

27 Federal regulations govern federal accounting, and this accounting system exceeds the scope of the book.

28 It is interesting to note that the Financial Accounting Foundation (FAF) funds and oversees both GASB and FASB.

29 Restricted donations are either permanent or temporary in nature. This text does not distinguish between the two categories.

30 The case illustration ignores the statement of cash flows.

31 There are other types of governmental type funds, such as trust and fiduciary funds. These funds are of lesser importance than expendable and nonexpendable funds, and their accounting exceeds the scope of this text.

32   Many pundits have noted the oxymoronic moniker.

33   Extended to its logical conclusion, the citizens of the city or county own its physical assets.

34   Contrast this to voluntary exchange (market) system where participants trade products for cash. An inverse relationship exists sometimes in an involuntary exchange system; non-taxpayers benefit from governmental services.

35   We assume a fiscal year that corresponds to the calendar year for the sake of simplicity. Most governments start their year on July 1.

36   We use the term *unreserved* fund balance because the fund can reserve a portion of its overall fund balance. The discussion on encumbrances in this chapter addresses this concept of *reserved* fund balances.

37   We introduce more technically correct terms than income statement and income later on in the chapter.

38   The city would depreciate the equipment over its expected life.

39   We assume that Redlands does not have a beginning fund balance.

40   The financial statements exclude the statement of cash flows.

41   It assumes Extreme Edge purchased both the customer database and the equipment at the beginning of the year and apportioned their costs equally over a five-year period.

Chapter 3

Auditing and Taxation

CHAPTER LEARNING OBJECTIVES

Upon completion of this chapter, readers should be able to:
- ➤ Understand the information contained in audit reports.
- ➤ Assess the ethical dilemmas inherent in auditing.
- ➤ Differentiate between the gross and net cost of debt financing.
- ➤ Incorporate the effective income tax rate into managerial decisions.
- ➤ Analyze deferred income tax liabilities and deferred income tax assets disclosures.
- ➤ Mitigate net operating losses by offsetting them against previous or future income.

We have examined the accounting process in both for-profit and not-for-profit sectors in the first two chapters of the text. An accounting system, however, extends beyond gathering financial data and reporting financial statements, which are internal processes. Accounting interacts with the external environment. This chapter explores these connections. Specifically, Chapter 3 investigates the primary contextual factors that affect entity accounting: audits and taxes. This chapter discusses the benefits managers derive from audited financial information. Independent verification of accounting outputs improves managerial decisions, due to the enhanced reliability of the accounting data. This chapter also explores how income taxes affect financial disclosures and how managers can use that knowledge to increase the effectiveness of their decisions.

Chapter 3 initially investigates the role of the audit function on corporate performance, financial disclosure, and decision-making. Managers who understand the value of audited data are better able to control operations, safeguard assets, and produce economically valid financial statements. The remainder of this chapter examines the affects of the principle regulatory cost of doing business—income taxes—on managerial decisions. It explains why managers should make decisions based upon actual tax consequences as opposed to their apparent costs. Further, it examines how managers adjust for differences between generally accepted accounting principles and income tax statutes.

AUDITING

The American Accounting Association defines **auditing** as "a systematic process of objectively obtaining and evaluating evidence regarding assertions about economic actions and events to ascertain the degree of correspondence between these assertions and established criteria and communicating the results to interested users."[1] Auditing is a specific form of **attestation**, which occurs when an individual renders an opinion about the conformity of something to something else, based on empirical evidence. An **audit**, therefore, measures specific financial results against GAAP (or an internally developed firm benchmark), and the **auditor** is one who conducts an audit.

Auditors may be firm employees or independent professionals who provide audit services for fees. Regardless of employment status, auditors should serve as unbiased, non-partisan, and independent evaluators of the extent to which the firm's economic events conform with established standards. An audit results in an **audit report**, which contains the **auditor's opinion**. Managers, as well as other vested parties such as investors, creditors, and regulators, include audit reports as critical informational inputs to their decision processes.

Audit reports focus on the accuracy and effectiveness of accounting systems because accounting measures and communicates financial information.[2] Internal auditors (firm employees) and external auditors (professional accounting firms) both play critical roles in insuring the accuracy and effectiveness of the accounting information system. Internal and external auditors serve interrelated, but different functions. Managers must appreciate both parties' contributions to the reliable compilation and communication of financial data. We now examine both types of audit functions in detail, beginning with the role of internal auditors.

INTERNAL AUDITS

Internal audit reports identify strengths, weaknesses, opportunities, and threats to an entity's accounting information system. **Internal auditors** assess the extent to which financial data conform to the expectations and standards established by management.[3] Firm employees functioning as internal auditors inform management where, when, and how the system lacks the controls necessary to produce relevant, reliable, and timely financial data. Internal auditors often act proactively in recommending corrections and improvements to the accounting system. Many of their recommendations are in the form of cost/benefit analyses. Internal auditors focus on improving organizational efficiency, as well as assessing its operational effectiveness.

Accounting data help control operational activities. **Internal control** assists in this task by defining the policies and procedures in the financial reporting system. The accounting system should insure that the firm records sales, collects cash, acquires resources, and pays its bills in an accurate and timely manner. Consequently, internal auditors establish and monitor the internal control elements designed to safeguard firm resources, process business transactions accurately, and issue timely financial reports.

The **Sarbanes-Oxley Act of 2002 (SOX)** requires management to report publicly its assessment of the firm's internal controls.[4] Both the chief executive officer and the chief financial officer sign **Management's Report on Internal Control**. In this report, management must attest to the effectiveness of the firm's policies and procedures related to financial record keeping, and their ability to identify unwarranted transactions.[5] Moreover, management must also identify deficiencies in the firm's internal control policies, and their potential effect on the financial statements. Due to public scrutiny of this disclosure, managers usually include in their report on internal control an outline of their plans to correct any significant control deficiencies.

Managerial decision-making requires numerous types of financial data; therefore, internal auditors should insure the firm maintains an accounting system that provides management with the needed information in useable formats. As we have noted in Chapters 1 and 2, managers make many decisions based on data that does not reflect the form or format of generally accepted accounting principles. For instance, we know that managers value cash flow data that may not conform to GAAP, in addition to accrual accounting information. Furthermore, they often consider cost behavior (e.g., fixed vs. variable costs), as opposed to cost format (e.g., cost of goods sold vs. operating expenses) when making production and sales decisions. Generally accepted accounting principles, which cover cost format, however, do not report how costs behave. In order to meet managerial needs therefore, the firm's accounting system must be adaptive enough to classify costs based on behavior as well as format.

Financial data flexibility is essential for managers to make sound decisions. Managers, consequently, must clearly communicate their financial data needs to their accountants. Internal audits help to meet this objective by measuring the extent to which the accounting system complies with managerial financial data requirements.

FINANCIAL STATEMENT (EXTERNAL) AUDITS

Performed by state-licensed members of public accounting firms (Certified Public Accountants or CPAs), **external auditors** render an independent opinion of the fairness of financial statements in conformity with generally accepted accounting principles. The target audiences for financial statement audit opinions are investors and creditors. These individuals have invested, or might invest, capital in the firm. As such, they need an unbiased opinion as to the fairness of an entity's financial statements in order to allocate their capital wisely. Unlike managers, however, equity investors and creditors do not have access to the operational activities of the firm, or the information contained within its accounting system. The independent audit report provides an unbiased assessment of management's financial assertions.

An independent audit is an expensive and time-consuming activity. Management can lower external audit costs through comprehensive and effective internal control policies and procedures, and timely internal financial audits. Thus, managers should develop comprehensive internal control policies and competent internal audit staffs in order to minimize external audit fees, and more importantly, insure accurate financial disclosures.

Management benefits from external audits in numerous ways. The external audit:

- Provides executives with an independent assessment of the organization's accounting system.
- Checks on the work conducted by internal auditors.
- Can validate that management is working on behalf of its shareholders (and not in its self-interest).
- Meets regulatory requirements, such as those mandated by the Securities and Exchange Commission.

There are seven important parts of a standard audit report. Every audit report contains the following information:

1. *Title*—Public company reports are required to begin with a title that references the "Independent Registered Public Accounting Firm." Reports for nonpublic companies may contain titles such as, "Independent Auditors Report," or "Report of the Independent Auditor."
2. *Addressee*—This is the individual, group, entity, board of directors, and/or stockholders who retained the services of the auditor.
3. *Introductory Paragraph*—This paragraph must state three things: financial statements covered by the report, that the statements

are the responsibility of management, and that the auditor has a responsibility to express an opinion.

4. *Scope Paragraph*—This paragraph states what is involved in the audit. For public companies, the auditor performs the engagement in accordance with the standards of the Public Company Accounting Oversight Board (PCAOB). An auditor of a nonpublic company conducts an audit in accordance with generally accepted auditing standards (GAAS). The scope paragraph must also state, "That the audit provides only reasonable assurance that the financial statements contain no material misstatements... that an audit involves an examination of evidence on a test basis...."

5. *Opinion Paragraph*—This paragraph expresses the auditor's opinion with regard to the fairness of the financial statements based upon evidence obtained through the audit.

6. *Name of Auditor*—The signature of the CPA firm that conducted the audit.

7. *Date of Report*—The auditor has completed all significant auditing procedures on this date.

Exhibit 3-1 presents the 2008 audit report for Coca-Cola as an example:

Exhibit 3-1
Audit Opinion

Report of the Independent Registered Public Accounting Firm

Board of Directors and Shareowners
The Coca-Cola Company

We have audited the accompanying consolidated balance sheets of The Coca-Cola Company and subsidiaries as of December 31, 2008 and 2007, and the related consolidated statements of income and cash flows for each of the three years ended December 31, 2008. These financial statements are the responsibility of the Company's management. Our responsibility is to express an opinion of these financial statements based on our audits.

We conducted our audits in accordance with the standards of the Public Company Accounting Oversight Board (United States). Those standards require that we plan and perform the audit to obtain reasonable assurance about whether the financial statements are free of material misstatement. An audit includes, examining, on a test basis, evidence supporting the amounts and disclosures in the financial statements. An audit also includes assessing the accounting principles used and significant estimates made by management, as well as evaluating the overall financial statement presentation. We believe that our audits provide a reasonable basis for our opinion.

In our opinion, the financial statements referred to above present fairly, in all material respects, the consolidated financial positions of The Coca-Cola Company and subsidiaries as of December 31, 2008 and 2007, and the related consolidated statements of income and cash flows for each of the three years ended December 31, 2008, in conformity with U.S. generally accepted accounting principles.

As discussed in Notes 1 and 17 to the consolidated financial statements, in 2007 the Company adopted FASB Interpretation No. 48 related to accounting for uncertainty in income taxes. Also as discussed in Notes 1 and 16 to the consolidated financial statements, in 2006 the Company adopted SFAS No. 158 related to defined benefit pension and other postretirement plans.

We have also audited, in accordance with the Public Company Accounting Oversight Board (United States), The Coca Cola Company's internal control over financial reporting as of December 31, 2008, based on criteria established in *Internal Control—Integrated Framework* issued by the Committee of Sponsoring Organizations of the Treadway Commission and our report dated February 26, 2009 expressed an unqualified opinion thereon.

(signed) Ernst & Young

Atlanta, Georgia
February 26, 2009

The critical portion of the audit report is the opinion paragraph (point 5 above and the third paragraph in Exhibit 3-1). External auditors render one of five audit opinions about the fairness of a company's financial statements based on GAAP. The types of **audit opinions** are as follows:

1. **Standard Unqualified Report.** The so-called *clean* audit opinion states that a company presents its financial statements fairly, in all material respects, in conformity with generally accepted accounting principles.
2. **Qualified Report—GAAP Departure.** A company whose financial statements depart in some material aspect from GAAP earns this

opinion. The opinion reads along the lines of "In our opinion, except for the GAAP departure, the financial statements present fairly...." As the language indicates, the auditors believe that the company presents its *overall* financial statements fairly, despite its departure from GAAP.

3. **Adverse Report.** If departures from GAAP are so pervasive that the reporting entities financial statements do not conform to GAAP, then auditors issue an adverse opinion.

4. **Qualified Report-Scope Limitation.** Auditors render this type of opinion when they are unable to obtain sufficient evidence about certain financial statement disclosures. For example, if auditors are unable to examine a portion of the company's inventory, the company may receive a qualified opinion, based on the limited scope of the audit. Similar to a GAAP departure qualification, auditors believe the firm reports its overall financial statements fairly, despite the scope limitation.

5. **Disclaimer of a Report.** Auditors who cannot determine the fairness of financial statements do not express an opinion. They disclaim an opinion, due to severe scope limitations encountered when conducting the audit.

Unqualified audit opinions, such as Coke received in 2008, validate the effectiveness of management's accounting system in addition to buoying investors' confidence in the reliability of the financial statements. Companies whose financial statements receive an adverse opinion or a disclaimer of an opinion signal managerial malfeasance.

Auditors add **explanatory language** to the report when a company receives anything but an unqualified opinion. These statements explain the matter of concern. In addition, the auditor may question a firm's ability to continue as a **going concern**. In such cases, auditors express doubt as to whether the company can continue operations indefinitely due to significant economic problems. Auditors can express this concern even if a company's financial statements conform to GAAP. This independent assessment of corporate sustainability calls management performance into question.

ETHICAL CONFLICTS AND AUDITING

Managers must be aware of the ethical conflicts posed by the attest function. The presumption is that external auditors render unbiased opinions about the fairness of financial statements, and internal auditors opine about numerous financial matters within the firm. One can question auditor independence, because firms pay for audits either directly or indirectly. Recall that internal auditors are firm employees, and companies contract (and pay) for external audit services. Conflicts can arise when management disagrees with audit opinions. The final portion of the audit section of Chapter 3 addresses the ethical dilemma confronting the firm and its audit functions, and it lists safeguards to auditor independence.

Companies may try to engage auditors who will issue unqualified audit opinions, regardless of the evidence generated by the audit procedures. This unethical practice is called **opinion shopping**. A quid pro quo arrangement can exist when companies shop for a clean audit report: the auditor meets management's expectations in return for future audit engagements (or other professional services).

Another form of opinion shopping occurs when a company knows their current auditor is going to qualify, disclaim, or issue an adverse opinion. In these instances, the firm cancels the existing audit engagement before the auditors issue their opinion. The unethical company then *shops* for another auditor who is willing to issue an unqualified opinion.

Numerous precautions now make it more difficult for a firm to opinion shop, and otherwise limit its ability to influence audit results. The safeguards include the following:

1. Firm notification to the Securities and Exchange Commission when changing auditors, and its reasons for doing so
2. Adherence to the code of professional ethics by CPAs (and severe penalties for code violations—including the loss of the CPA license)
3. Stricter oversight of the auditing profession by the Public Company Accounting Oversight Board
4. Mandated periodic rotation of audit partners
5. Virtual elimination of non-audit services performed for a client by its auditor

The Sarbanes-Oxley Act of 2002 mandates points three, four, and five in the above list. This sweeping legislation was the federal government's response to numerous financial reporting failures in the early part of the twenty-first century, most notably that of the Enron Corporation. Other key aspects of SOX include whistle-blower protection for both internal and external auditors, and the requirement that management asserts in writing that its financial statements are accurate and free of material misstatement. SOX mandates strict civil, and sometimes criminal, penalties for firms that violate the law.

Much of the recent controversy surrounding the (perceived) failure of the audit function is attributable to the existence of an **expectations gap**.

Accountants define this gap as the difference between the public's perception of the attest function and the auditors view of the job. The public, including many managers and regulators, assume that auditors guarantee the accuracy of the financial statements, and therefore detect all instances of financial fraud. Auditors' view their job as rendering an opinion as to the conformity of the financial statements with GAAP. They derive that opinion, in turn, based on sampled evidence. Time and cost constraints prohibit auditors from proving the accuracy of every business transaction.

One benefit from financial debacles such as Enron is a marked reduction in this expectations gap. Auditors must comply with stricter audit-related statutes, and further threats of greater government involvement in the profession. Consequently, auditors have increased their audit procedures, become more vigilant about detecting fraud, and reestablished auditor independence. Similarly, market participants are now more aware of the inherent limitations of the audit function. Furthermore, they are more acutely aware that corporate financial disclosures are the assertions of the firm, and not the auditor's representations. Management is responsible for producing financial statements that conform to generally accepted accounting principles. This obligation is but one of many assumed by managers who act as financial stewards on behalf of corporate shareholders.

Conforming to GAAP, contracting with auditors, and complying with SOX are all regulatory tasks that managers must address. The greatest regulatory burden, however, is adhering to the financial costs imposed by governmental agencies. We now turn our attention to the tax consequences of engaging in commerce.

Income Taxes

Income taxes are a cost of doing business, and managers must include them along with other expenses in their decision-making processes. Unlike other business costs, however, **income tax expenses** have two unique characteristics. First, firm financial performance determines its income tax expense. As such, income tax expense derives from the difference between an entity's revenues and its business costs. Second, statutory laws, and not generally accepted accounting principles, govern the firm's income tax obligation. Managers must incorporate both of these features into their economic decisions. The unique characteristics of income tax affect performance assessment, effective income tax rates, and the timing of cash flows. We now examine these three income-tax-related issues in turn.

PERFORMANCE ASSESSMENT

Expenses shield a portion of revenue from taxation. In other words, business costs reduce the amount of earnings that taxing authorities, such as the U.S. government, can claim from an entity. This factor reduces a firm's cost of debt financing, and could affect its evaluation of managerial performance. The deductibility of financing charges effectively reduces the firm's **effective cost of debt financing**. We demonstrate this point in the following example.

Assume that Redlands, Inc. began business operations with $200,000 of equity financing. The firm's one department (Department A) made a single product that served one market. Redlands then formed Department B by borrowing $200,000 at 10% and began manufacturing a second product with assets acquired from the borrowed funds.[6] We will further assume that these two departments were equal in their operating performances. Exhibit 3-2 contains the relevant financial results:

Exhibit 3-2
Equity versus Debt Financing (in thousands)

Income Statement	Department A	Department B
Revenues	$100	$100
Cost of goods sold	40	40
Gross profit	60	60
Operating expenses	30	30
Interest expense (10% of $200)	---	20
Pretax income	30	10
Income tax expense (40%)	12	4
Net department income	$18	$6

Note that Department B's net income is only $12,000 less than that of Department A ($6,000 versus $18,000), despite its interest expense of $20,000. That financing charge effectively shields $20,000 of Department B's revenues from taxation, allowing taxing authorities to claim only 40% of $10,000 and not 40% of $30,000. Consequently, interest expense shields a portion of revenues from taxation and reduces the firm's effective cost of borrowing. One computes the effective cost of debt as interest expense multiplied by one minus the income tax rate. The cost of debt financing for the firm (or specifically Department B in this case) is therefore 6% ($12,000 / $200,000), and not 10% ($20,000 / $200,000).

Managers make future investment decisions based on the effective, or net, cost of debt, and not gross financing charges. For example, the managers of both Department A and B may have potential investment opportunities. They should evaluate the expected future cash flow from such investments against the firm's effective 6% debt financing charge and not the 10% stated rate of debt financing.[7]

Net financing charges can also affect managerial compensation. Refer to the data in Exhibit 3-2, and assume that Redlands pays a bonus of 10% of net income to its divisional managers. The manager of Department B would receive a $1,200 lower bonus than that received by the manager of Department A ($600 vs. $1,800). The method of departmental financing, rather than operating performance, produced the bonus differential. Clearly, this bonus arrangement is unfair, and it could cause dysfunctional managerial behavior.

Firms insure fair managerial compensation by adjusting for the interdepartmental difference in debt financing. One means of doing so is to adjust the **return on assets (ROA)** ratio. One computes the unadjusted ROA ratio as follows: net income / total assets. ROA is the product of two ratios, which are **net profit margin** (net income / sales revenues) and **asset turnover** (sales revenues / total assets).[8]

You adjust ROA by adding each department's net interest expense to its net income. The *adjusted* net income affects a department's net profit margin and its overall return on assets. Exhibit 3-3 presents the debt-financing adjusted return on asset calculations for Departments A and B listed in Exhibit 3-2:

Exhibit 3-3
Adjusted Return on Assets (dollar amounts in thousands)

Income Statement	Department A	Department B
Net income	$18	$6
Unadjusted profit margin	$18 / $100 = 18%	$6 / $100 = 6%
Asset turnover	$100 / $200 = .5	$100 / $200 = .5
Unadjusted return on assets	$18 / $200 = 9%	$6 / $200 = 3%
Interest expense	$0	$20
Net (effective) interest expense	0	($20 * [1 - .40]) = $12
Adjusted profit margin	$18 / $100 = 18%	($6+12) / $100 = 18%
Asset turnover	$100 / $200 = .5	$100 / $200 = .5
Adjusted return on assets	$18 / $200 = 9%	($6+12) / $200 = 9%

The adjusted return on assets data from Exhibit 3-3 demonstrates that the manager of Department B performed as well as his or her Department A counterpart on a debt-adjusted basis.

EFFECTIVE INCOME TAX RATES

Financial statements must conform to GAAP; consequently, accounting systems process data on the accrual basis of accounting. (Recall that under accrual accounting, an entity recognizes revenues when earned and matches expenses to them, regardless of the timing of their cash flows.) Corporations pay income taxes based upon taxable income. The Internal Revenue Code, not GAAP, determines the amount of taxable income.[9] Tax accounting, as opposed to financial accounting, is rooted in cash receipts and disbursements. Consequently, **income taxes payable** are a function of cash-based, and not accrual-based, earnings.[10]

Two issues arise from the difference between GAAP and the income tax code—permanent and temporary (or timing) differences. A **permanent income tax difference** occurs when either GAAP or tax regulations permit a revenue or expense recognition item, but the other authority does not. Permanent differences alter the actual (or true) cost of the entity's income tax expense. For example, assume that a firm reported pretax income of $300,000 on a GAAP basis, but $50,000 of that amount resulted from interest on municipal bond investments. Its taxable income would only be $250,000 because the Internal Revenue Code excludes interest received on municipal bonds from taxable income. If we assume that the statutory income tax rate is 40%, then the firm would owe the government $100,000 for taxes ($250,000 * .4). It would also report only $100,000 of income tax expense on its GAAP income statement instead of $120,000 ($300,000 * .4).

Permanent differences alter an entity's **effective income tax rate.**[11] One divides income tax expense by financial (GAAP) pretax income to compute the effective income tax rate. For the above example, the permanent difference lowers the firm's statutory income tax rate of 40% to an effective rate of 33.3% ($100,000 / $300,000). Managers use the *effective* income tax rate, and not the *statutory* income tax rate, when adjusting for the cost of debt financing and return on assets.

CASH FLOW

Temporary (or timing) income tax differences are the second way that GAAP differs from tax regulations. These types of differences arise because GAAP and tax accounting recognize certain amounts of revenues and expenses in different reporting periods. Unlike permanent differences, however, temporary income tax differences do not result in an *aggregate* income differential. Instead, the timing differences between GAAP and tax reporting rules affect *periodic* financial disclosures. The following example and exhibit demonstrates the financial statement effects of a temporary income tax difference.

We assume that Redlands, Inc. began business in 2009. Its consistent revenues and expenses result in an annual net income of $40,000 in both 2009 and 2010 under generally accepted accounting principles. The firm did not collect $30,000 of its 2009 sales until 2010. Redlands collected all of its 2010 sales in that year as well as the outstanding $30,000 2009 accounts receivable. We further assume that Redlands paid all of its operating expenses in cash as incurred, and the statutory (and effective) income tax rate is 40%. Tax law dictates that taxable income results from the difference between cash collected from sales and cash paid for expenses.

Exhibit 3-4 presents the pertinent annual and cumulative financial statement disclosures under generally accepted accounting principles.

Exhibit 3-4
Temporary Income Tax Difference (in thousands)

	2009	2010	Two Year Total
Income Statements			
Revenues	$200	$200	$400
Operating expenses	160	160	320
Pretax income	40	40	80
Income tax expense—current	4	28	
Income tax expense—deferred	12	(12)	
Total income tax expense	16	16	32
Net income	$24	$24	$48
Balance Sheets—December 31			
Assets:			
Accounts receivable	$30	$0	
Liabilities:			
Deferred income tax payable	$12	$0	
Statements of Cash Flow			
Cash paid for income taxes	$4	$28	$32

Note from the income statement portion of Exhibit 3-4 that pretax (GAAP-based) income is $40,000 in both years. The 2009 *taxable* income, however, is only $10,000 ($170,000 of *cash* revenues minus operating expenses of $160,000). The collection of the 2009 receivables in 2010 results in 2010 taxable income of $70,000 ($230,000 cash collected from revenues minus the $160,000 operating expenses). Consequently, Redlands is obligated to pay $4,000 for income taxes to the government in 2009 ($10,000 * .4) and $28,000 in the following year ($70,000 * .4). Exhibit 3-4 also presents these cash payment amounts in the company's cash flow statements.[12]

Redlands recognizes $16,000 of accrual-based income tax expense in both 2009 and 2010. The firm defers payment in 2009 of $12,000 of its $16,000 total 2009 income tax expense until 2010 when it actually collects its outstanding accounts receivable. This creates a **deferred income tax liability** of $12,000 that Redlands reports on its 2009 balance sheet ($30,000 in deferred revenue times .40).[13] The reader should note that the process reverses in 2010. Redlands $28,000 payment for income taxes in that year covers its $16,000 of income tax expense for 2010 and eliminates its 2009 income tax liability stemming from the 2009 income tax deferral.

Temporary income tax differences have three important interrelated considerations for managers. First, unlike permanent income tax differences, timing differences *do not* affect the effective income tax rate. Note that total income tax expense (current adjusted for deferred) is $16,000 in both 2009 and 2010, and annual pretax income equals $40,000. This results in a 40% effective income tax rate ($16,000 / $40,000) in each year, which matches the statutory percentage. Second, temporary differences reverse themselves over time.[14] The reader should note that both financial reporting and taxable income equal $80,000 over the two-year period, and that Redlands eliminated its deferred income tax liability by December 31, 2010. Third, the firm conserves cash when it can defer payment on a portion of its income tax expense. Recall from Exhibit 3-4 that Redlands paid only $4,000 in cash for taxes in 2009.

Reducing current income tax payments is sound management practice, due to the opportunity cost of cash and the time value of money.[15] In other words, it is in management's best interest not to pay taxes until it is necessary to do so. Certain accounting rules can create temporary income tax differences that allow managers to conserve cash. They do so because, in addition to its cash-based focus, tax regulations allow firms to time certain deductible expenses differently than GAAP. The most prominent difference centers on depreciable assets. A firm can accelerate tax depreciation while depreciating those same assets on a straight-line basis for financial reporting purposes.[16] Accelerated depreciation shields a greater amount of revenues from taxation in the early years of an asset's life, thereby deferring cash payments for taxes until the latter years of asset life. Consequently, managers can use that retained cash for producing wealth.

Managers must also be aware that **net operating losses** affect cash flow. Such a loss occurs when tax-deductible expenses exceed taxable revenues in a given reporting period. Companies can use one period's loss to offset taxable income from previous years, or apply it against the earnings of future periods. The former strategy defines a **loss carryback**, and people refer to the latter as a **loss carryforward**.[17]

Data from Extreme Edge, this text's hypothetical Internet retailer, illustrate the benefits of a net operating loss. Notice from the Exhibit 2-1 income statements in Chapter 2 that the company reported a 2011 pretax loss of $15,000. Its income tax expense in that year was a negative $6,000, which one defines more precisely as a $6,000 **income tax benefit**. That income tax benefit reduced the $15,000 pretax loss to a $9,000 net loss. Now refer to the Exhibit's 2010 and 2011 balance sheets. The earlier year reported $6,000 in income tax payable (because the firm only paid $10,000 of its $16,000 income tax obligation for 2010). The 2011 balance sheet, however, did not report any tax obligation. What occurred was that Extreme Edge carried its 2011 net operating loss back one year and eliminated its existing income tax debt. By satisfying the 2010 income tax obligation with the next year's loss carryback, Extreme Edge did not have to pay the government $6,000 cash for the unpaid portion of its 2010 income tax obligation.

Summary

Chapter 3 examined the relationship between an entity's accounting system and its external environment. The first section of the chapter explored the role of the audit, or attest, function. Firms employ internal auditors to insure compliance with the firm's policies and procedures. An independent accounting firm serves as the entity's external auditor. The function of the external auditor is to render an opinion as to the fairness of the firm's financial statements in accordance with generally accepted accounting principles. Both internal and external auditors should work independently of management. The fact that the firm pays its auditors, however, can create ethical conflicts between the entity and its auditors.

The second portion of this chapter investigated how income taxes affect financial reporting and managerial decisions. Laws, rather than generally accepted accounting principles, determine income tax liability. This difference creates both permanent and temporary income tax differences for the firm. The former difference affects the entity's effective income tax rate, while the latter type creates deferred income tax assets and liabilities. In addition, a firm that incurs operating losses can carry the loss back in time or into the future, in order to offset income.

Key Terms

Adverse Report
Asset turnover
Attestation
Audit
Audit opinions
Audit report
Auditing
Auditor
Auditor's opinion
Deferred income
Disclaimer of a Report
Effective cost of debt
Effective income tax rate
Expectations gap
Explanatory language
External auditors
Going concern
Income tax benefit
Income tax expenses
Income taxes payable
Internal audit reports
Internal auditors
Internal control
Loss carryback
Loss carryforward
Management's Report on Internal Control
Net operating losses
Net profit margin
Opinion shopping
Permanent income tax difference
Qualified Report—GAAP Departure
Qualified Report-Scope Limitation
Return on assets (ROA)
Sarbanes-Oxley Act of 2002
Standard Unqualified Report
Temporary (or timing) income tax differences

Assignments

Accounting Concepts Crossword

Across

¹ When a company uses one period's loss to offset taxable income from previous years.

² An individual who renders an independent opinion on the fairness of financial statements in conformity with GAAP.

³ The so-called *clean* audit opinion states that a company presents its financial statements fairly, in all material respects, in conformity with GAAP.

⁴ Timing differences that arise because GAAP and tax accounting recognize certain amounts of revenues and expenses in different reporting periods.

Down

¹ A company employee who assesses the extent to which financial data conform to the expectations and standards established by management.

² If departures from GAAP are so pervasive that the reporting entity's financial statements do not conform to GAAP, and then auditors issue this opinion.

³ A systematic process of objectively obtaining and evaluating evidence regarding assertions about economic actions and events to ascertain the degree of correspondence between these assertions and established criteria and communicating the results to interested users.

⁴ Act that requires management to report publicly its assessment of the firms internal controls.

DISCUSSION ITEMS

What Would Your Accountant Say?

Perhaps the most contentious aspect of the Sarbanes-Oxley Act of 2002 is Section 404, which requires management to report on the adequacy of the company's internal controls over financial reporting. The CEO of your company has asked you to define the phrase "internal control," to describe broadly the type of controls that might exist within your organization, and to catalog the specific controls that exist in your department. What would your accountant say to the CEO?

Theory vs. Practice

This chapter generally describes the roles and responsibilities assumed by an organization's internal and external auditors. In theory, internal auditors are responsible for assessing the extent to which financial data conform to the expectations and standards established by management, and external auditors render an independent opinion of the fairness of financial statements in conformity with generally accepted accounting principles. In practice, however, both internal and external auditors often provide services to an organization that go far beyond these limited descriptions. Use your own background and work experience to describe some of the services you have seen performed by internal and external auditors that go beyond the general roles described above.

PROBLEMS

Problem 3-1

Redlands, Inc. consists of three departments: Ontario, Riverside, and Burbank. It financed Ontario, the newest department, with an 8% bond. Redlands financed Riverside and Burbank, its older two departments, with shareholders investments. Each department reports revenues, net income, and total assets as follows:

Item	Ontario	Riverside	Burbank
Total assets	$200,000	$300,000	$500,000
Net income	11,000	22,000	41,000
Sales revenues	300,000	400,000	600,000

In addition, Redlands has a 25% income tax rate.

Required:

Rank order the three departments' performance on a tax-adjusted return on asset basis. Discuss whether your decision would have differed if you did not consider income taxes.

Problem 3-2

The Temecula Company reports the following financial (GAAP-based) income statement (in thousands).

Revenues	$600
Cost of goods sold	240
Gross profit	360
Selling expenses	110
Administrative expenses	90
Operating income	160
Financial (interest) expense	50
Pretax financial income	$110

In addition, Temecula has three income-tax-related issues and a 40% income tax rate:

- As part of its administrative expenses, the firm included a $40,000 fine paid to the Environmental Protection Agency for a polluting a river near its operations. The Internal Revenue Code does not allow companies to deduct fines paid to a governmental agency.
- Temecula made cash sales and paid *most* of its operating expenses in cash. The firm has yet to pay $5,000 related to its selling expenses. Tax authorities allow firms to deduct expenses only when firms pay for them.
- The company included $20,000 of depreciation expense in the category of selling expenses. Temecula accelerated depreciation for tax purposes; therefore, it deducted $30,000 of depreciation for tax purposes.

Required:

1. Determine *taxable* income.
2. Compute income taxes payable.
3. Determine financial (GAAP) net income.
4. Calculate the effective income tax rate.

5. Present the effect of income taxes on this year's statement of cash flows.

6. Disclose the deferred income tax accounts on the balance sheet.

Case 3-1

Beginning in 2009, you become the chief financial officer of General Motors Corporation (GM). The company's board of directors has asked you to inform the audit committee about the pending audit opinion of Deloitte & Touche, LLP. The audit committee, in turn, will report to the board about the findings of GM's external audit firm.

The independent audit opinion contains both good news and bad news: Deloitte & Touche believe that GM's financial statements conformed to generally accepted accounting principles. On the other hand, the audit firm has expressed concern about the automaker's ability to continue as a viable economic entity (going concern). The relevant information from the pending audit opinion is as follows:

> In our opinion, such consolidated financial statements present fairly in all material respects, the financial position of General Motors Corporation and subsidiaries at December 31, 2008 and 2007, and the results of their operations and their cash flows for each of the three years in the period ended December 31, 2008, in conformity with accounting principles generally accepted in the United States of America.
>
> The accompanying consolidated financial statements for the year have been prepared assuming that the Corporation will continue as a going concern. As discussed in Note 2 to the consolidated financial statements, the Corporation's recurring losses from operations, stockholders' deficit, and inability to generate sufficient cash flow to meet its obligations and sustain operations raise substantial doubt about its ability to continue as a going concern. Management's plans concerning these matters are also discussed in Note 2 to the consolidated financial statements. The consolidated financial statements do not include any adjustments that might result from the outcome of this uncertainty.

The auditors' explanatory paragraph independently verified GM's grave financial situation. As CFO, you note that the firm has

-   $71 billion of net losses from 2006 through 2008
-   a retained deficit of $86 billion as of December 31, 2008

- used more than $12 billion in cash from operating activities than it generated in 2008

These distressing financial figures enumerate GM's poor performance over many decades. The causes that produced these results are varied and numerous. Without affixing blame, you recall GM's:

- Inability to protect market share
- Lack of product innovations
- Deficient product quality
- Bloated cost structure
- Ineffective management

As the audit report alludes, GM now teeters on the verge of bankruptcy. Although your charge is to inform the audit committee about the pending audit opinion, you are sure they will engage you about the larger financial crisis facing the company. You know that the audit committee will seek information about the possibility of the firm filing for bankruptcy protection under Chapter 11 of the U.S. Bankruptcy Code. This filing would allow the courts to supervise GM's reorganization and reemergence into the marketplace.

You review the critical items that would occur under bankruptcy. Foremost among the positive aspects of bankruptcy protection is that GM would have the opportunity to void contracts and renegotiate debt obligations. Bankruptcy would allow the company to eliminate onerous labor contracts, which place it at competitive disadvantage. The firm could then establish a wage structure equivalent to other car manufacturers. GM could also reduce its huge retirement benefit obligations. Legacy costs for pension payments and health benefits to former employees have long consumed substantial amounts of company cash. GM could also shutter nonproductive plants and cancel long-term leases. The court would also make creditors negotiate existing debt obligations. This would result in the firm settling many financial obligations for pennies on the dollar, or converting debt into equity stakes of the restructured firm.

You also contemplate the disadvantages to bankruptcy protection as well. The court-appointed bankruptcy trustee would have to approve all major corporate decisions. Thus, the judiciary, rather than management, would effectively run the firm during bankruptcy proceedings. In addition, bankruptcy would increase administrative costs substantially. General Motors would have to pay for the legion of attorneys, accountants, and other consultants assisting in the corporate restructuring.

Market reaction to a bankruptcy filing by GM has more serious consequences than loss of managerial autonomy and increased administrative costs in your opinion. You assess whether consumers will lose trust in the firm's ability to deliver vehicles, service them, and honor warranties. If customers desert the firm in substantial numbers, then you worry that the bankruptcy reorganization will become a corporate liquidation.

Required:

Prepare a one-page opening statement addressed to the audit committee. In addition to your opening statement, anticipate three questions that the committee will ask you and draft your responses.

Endnotes

1   Committee on Basic Auditing Concepts, a Statement of Basic Auditing Concepts, (Sarasota, FL: AAA, 1973), p.2

2   Other types of audits exist, such as efficiency audits, but they exceed the scope of this text.

3   Variance analysis discussed in Chapter 7 is an example of internal auditing.

4   Firms make this disclosure as part of their annual Form 10-K report filed with the Securities and Exchange Commission.

5   Section 404 of the Sarbanes-Oxley Act of 2002.

6   We greatly simplify the concept of firm financing by attributing debt financing costs to a single unit within an entity. The intent of this text is to demonstrate effective interest rates and evaluate its affect on managerial performance assessment. We develop this concept in Chapter 4.

7   This decision assumes that the marginal cost of capital remains at 10% and the income tax rate is stable at 40%.

8   Note that the sales revenues terms cancel one another out (the denominator in net profit margin and numerator in asset turnover). This offset results in net income / total assets, which is the return on assets ratio.

9   Corporations may also pay income taxes to states and municipalities. They conform to state and city income tax codes in such instances.

10   Tax codes require a *modified* cash basis, as opposed to a *strict* cash basis, because the cost of certain items, such as fixed assets, is not fully deductible in the year acquired. Tax filers, in essence, treat those items on an accrual basis by recognizing tax-deductible depreciation over the asset's useful life.

11   Although this discussion lowers the firm's effective income tax rate, other types of permanent differences can increase it.

12 This statement assumes that Redlands pays its obligation in cash. If it does not do so by the end of the year, the firm would report an income taxes payable liability on its balance sheet.

13 Technically, deferred income tax expense results from accounts receivable and its related income tax liability and not the other way around. We present the concept of temporary differences from an income statement orientation, rather than a balance sheet point of reference, in order to simplify student learning.

14 The firm, however, could originate new temporary income tax differences as others reverse. Financial statements report the cumulative net effect of all temporary income tax differences.

15 We will develop this topic in Chapter 4.

16 The Internal Revenue Code allows firms to employ the Modified Accelerated Cost Recovery System (MACRS) of depreciation for tax purposes. The extent to which firms can accelerate depreciation is subject to statute and the law changes over time to meet the economic (and sometimes political) objectives.

17 Economic fairness underlies the rationale for carryforward and carrybacks. Government taxes companies when they create wealth; therefore, they compensate them when operations reduce wealth. You should also note that tax regulations limit the number of years in which firms can carryforward or carryback a net operating loss.

Chapter 4

Accounting for Entity Capitalization

CHAPTER LEARNING OBJECTIVES

Upon completion of this chapter, readers should be able to:
- ➤ Account for corporate debt and equity financing.
- ➤ Analyze transactions that expand and contract shareholders' equity.
- ➤ Incorporate time value of money concepts into long-term liability accounting.
- ➤ Articulate how bond discounts and premiums affect financial statement disclosures.
- ➤ Utilize the weighted average cost of capital as an input for making decisions.

A balance sheet reports entity resources and claims to those resources. This statement of financial position enumerates where the organization secured its financing and how it invested those funds. Entity assets enable the organization to meet its mission, be it creating wealth for a profit-seeking firm or serving society as a not-for-profit enterprise. In other words, an organization invests in resources that allow it to conduct operations. Lenders and owners (or donors in the case of non-profits) provide the capital that enables the entity to acquire the resources necessary to meet organizational goals. This chapter examines the means by which a firm acquires capital, and how it accounts for those contributions. It also measures the costs of entity financing.

A firm must acquire capital in order to begin operations. It may supplement those initial cash infusions with additional debt issues and stock offerings as needed throughout its life. Chapter 4 focuses on accounting for the capital financing needs of for-profit firms. As such, this chapter explores accounting for equity (owner) financing, as opposed to accounting for taxpayer financing of governments and contributor funding of voluntary not-for-profit organizations.[1] Chapter 4 investigates accounting for debt financing, after it explores equity accounting. We conclude this chapter by examining how one uses accounting data to determine the individual cost of debt and equity financing, and the combined cost of capital.

ACCOUNTING FOR EQUITY

We begin our discussion of equity financing by defining numerous terms that underlie corporate accounting. Once you understand the relevant terminology, we explain the accounting process for stock transactions, and their affect on financial disclosures. We conclude this section of the chapter by examining how corporate dividends affect accounting disclosures.

EQUITY TERMS

Corporate charters **authorize** the firm to sell a certain number of shares. **Issued shares** are the number of **authorized shares** that the firm actually sells. At times, the entity may purchase some of its issued shares in the open market from investors and place those shares in the corporate treasury. The firm can either reissue or retire these so-called **treasury shares**. Accountants refer to the difference between issued shares and currently held shares in the treasury as **outstanding shares**.

All corporations issue **common stock**, and some sell **preferred shares**.[2] Befitting the name, preferred shareholders receive cash dividends before the firm distributes them to common stockholders. Preferred stockholders also receive a return of their investment before common stockholders in the event of a corporate liquidation.[3] Preferred stock, however, does not vote in corporate matters; only the common shareholders can exercise the voting franchise. By controlling the firm and receiving wealth distributions after preferred shareholders, common stockholders reap the largest rewards of corporate success and bear the greatest risk of corporate failure. In essence, common shareholders are the ultimate risk investors in for-profit ventures.

Both preferred and common stock have a par (or stated) value, which is set forth in the corporate charter. **Par (or stated) value** represents the minimum selling price of a share of stock when the firm issues it. Obviously, companies issue stock at its prevailing market price, which usually exceeds par value. **Additional paid-in-capital in excess of par value** defines the difference between share sale price and its par value.

A firm accounts for treasury stock purchases at cost (i.e., market price at the time of acquisition). If the entity subsequently reissues treasury stock, it does so at current market prices. In the event the sale price of treasury stock exceeds its acquisition cost, the firm creates (or increases) an account called

additional paid in capital on treasury stock transactions. If the firm sells treasury shares at less than acquisition cost, it decreases the account of additional paid in capital on treasury stock transactions. (The firm would decrease retained earnings if an additional paid in capital on treasury stock account did not exist.)

EQUITY TRANSACTIONS

In order to illustrate equity accounting, we assume that Redland, Inc. engages in the following equity transactions during 2010, its first year of business:

1. Issued 100 shares of common stock with a $1 par value for $7 per share
2. Issued 50 shares of preferred stock with a $2 par value for $10 per share
3. Issued 40 shares of common stock in exchange for a parcel of land with a $240 market value
4. Purchased 30 shares of treasury stock for $5 per share
5. Sold 10 shares of treasury stock for $8 per share
6. Sold another 10 shares of treasury stock for $4 per share

Exhibit 4-1 present the journal entries for Redlands' stock transactions.

Exhibit 4-1
General Journal

Trans.	Accounts	Debit	Credit
1	Cash (100 * $7)	700	
	Common stock (100 * $1)		100
	Additional paid in capital in excess of par, common stock		600
2	Cash (50 * $10)	500	
	Preferred stock (50 * $2)		100
	Additional paid in capital in excess of par, preferred stock		400
3	Land (40 * $6)	240	
	Common stock (40 * $1)		40
	Additional paid in capital in excess of par, common stock		200

4	Treasury stock, common (30 * $5)	150	
	Cash		150
5	Cash (10 * $8)	80	
	Treasury stock, common (10 * $5)		50
	Additional paid in capital, common treasury stock (10 * $3)		30
6	Cash (10 * $4)	40	
	Additional paid in capital, common treasury stock (10 * $1)	10	
	Treasury stock, common (10 * $5)		50

Exhibit 4-2 presents the shareholders' equity section of Redlands December 31, 2010 balance sheet based on the above journal entries. (Exhibit 4-2 assumes Redlands earned $300 of net income in 2010.)

Exhibit 4-2
Shareholders' Equity

Preferred stock, $2 par, 50 shares issued and outstanding	$100
Common stock, $1 par, 140 shares issued and 10 shares held in treasury	140
Total stock issued at par value	240
Additional paid in capital in excess of par, preferred stock	400
Additional paid in capital in excess of par, common stock	800
Additional paid in capital, common treasury stock	20
Total contributed capital	1,460
Retained earnings	300
Less: treasury stock, 10 common shares	(50)
Total shareholders' equity	**$1,710**

DIVIDENDS

Investors purchase shares of stock in anticipation of realizing capital gains and receiving dividends. They realize a **capital gain** when the current price of a share of stock exceeds its acquisition cost. As noted earlier in this text, a dividend occurs when the firm distributes a portion of its earnings to its shareholders. A **dividend** is a return on investment to the shareowner. Companies declare dividends before the date that they distribute cash to their shareholders.[4] The **dividend declaration date** establishes the corporate liability, the **dividend**

date of record establishes ownership of the shares receiving the dividend, and the firm settles that obligation on the **dividend payment date**.

Assume from the above example that Redlands, Inc. declared a 10% preferred dividend toward the end of 2010 and paid the dividend at year-end. Concurrent with the preferred dividend, the firm declared and paid a 10% common dividend. The common dividend events occurred after Redlands sold its second pool of treasury stock. Exhibit 4-3 presents these dividend transactions:

Exhibit 4-3
General Journal

Trans.	Accounts	Debit	Credit
7	Retained earnings ($2 par * .10 * 50 shares)	10	
	Dividends payable—preferred stock		10
8	Retained earnings ($1 par * .10 * 130 shares)	13	
	Dividends payable—common stock		13
9	Dividends payable—preferred stock	10	
	Cash		10
10	Dividends payable—common stock	13	
	Cash		13

The reader should note three important items from Exhibit 4-3:

1. Dividends are a function of the stock's par value. Additional paid in capital in excess of par does *not* affect dividend amounts.
2. A firm only declares and pays a dividend on *outstanding* shares of stock (i.e., issued shares less treasury shares). Examine how the common dividend equals $13 in Exhibit 4-3. This amount occurs because Redlands declared the common dividend when it held 10 shares of common stock in its treasury, and therefore had 130 shares of outstanding common stock.[5]
3. The entity reduces retained earnings when it *declares* dividends and not when it *pays* them. Dividend payments merely settle the firm's outstanding liability to its shareholders. While dividend payments do not affect retained earnings, the manager must bear in mind that they do reduce the firm's cash balance. Consequently, the company

reports the *payment* of the dividends as a reduction of cash in the financing activities section of its statement of cash flows.

Exhibit 4-4 presents both the statement of shareholders' equity for 2010 and the shareholders' equity section of the balance sheet on December 31, 2010, after Redlands declared and paid a dividend to its preferred and common shareholders:

Exhibit 4-4
Statement of Shareholders' Equity

Beginning retained earnings	$ 0
Net income	300
Dividends declared	(23)
Ending retained earnings	$277

Shareholders' Equity—Balance Sheet

Preferred stock, $2 par, 50 shares issued and outstanding	$100
Common stock, $1 par, 140 shares issued and 10 shares held in treasury	140
Total stock issued at par value	240
Additional paid in capital in excess of par, preferred stock	400
Additional paid in capital in excess of par, common stock	800
Additional paid in capital, common treasury stock	20
Total contributed capital	1,460
Retained earnings	277
Less: treasury stock, 10 common shares	(50)
Total shareholders' equity	**$1,687**

ACCOUNTING FOR DEBT

The alternative to equity financing is creditor, or debt financing. We now turn our attention to the accounting for borrowed funds. We examine only the accounting for long-term financial obligations. We ignore current liabilities because they arise from business operations, and the firm uses cash generated from current assets to settle such obligations. In order to account for long-term debt, however, one must comprehend the time value of money concept. We begin our discussion about debt accounting in this area and then proceed to processing debt-related transactions.

TIME VALUE CONCEPT

A dollar today is worth more than a dollar in the future. This axiom has economic validity because of the **time value of money**. Money has time value because one can invest a current sum of money and earn interest on it. Consequently, a future monetary amount is not as valuable as it is when measured in today's dollars. The time value of money affects long-term debt accounting because firms borrow money in the present and repay it in the future.[6] The borrowing entity may not settle these long-term obligations for ten or twenty years (or longer) in the future. Inasmuch as the firm must record the liability in its accounting records currently (when it borrows the money), its accounting system must reflect the current value of the liability. Accountants refer to recording such transactions at the **present value** of the liability. **Discounting** is the process of converting a future amount of cash to its present value.

Mathematical formulas exist that allow one to compute the present value equivalent of a future amount (or amounts) of money. As a practical matter, individuals use present value tables or financial calculators to discount future cash flow. We will use present value tables for our discussion in Chapter 4. (Appendix B located toward the end of the text presents the table values.) A **present value table** contains an array of present value table factors. A **present value table factor** represents a combination of an interest rate (i) and a number of time periods (n). One determines the present value of a future amount of money by multiplying the future value of money by the applicable present value table factor.

Two types of present value computations exist: **single (lump) sum of money** conversions, and multiple sums of money conversions. An **annuity** defines the latter process, and it assumes equal cash **rents** (payments in the case of a liability) that occur at equal times in the future. One computes the present value of a future amount of cash (single sum) as follows:

Future amount of cash * single sum present value factor = present value of cash.

For example, assume that Redlands, Inc. promised to pay $2,000 for a three-year borrowing on December 31, 2012. The annual interest rate was ten percent (10%) when Redlands received cash and incurred the liability on January 1, 2010.[7] The amount of money that Redlands would receive today (the present value of the liability) is as follows:

$$\$2,000 * .751 = \$1,502$$

One finds the .751 present value factor as the cell that reflects the 3 period column (n) and the 10% interest rate row (i) in the present value of 1 table.

Alternatively, assume that Redlands agrees to pay $2,000 annually beginning on December 31, 2010 in exchange for a sum of money on January 1, 2010. The amount of money that Redlands would receive today (the present value of the *annuity*); assuming a 10% interest rate is as follows:

$$\$2,000 * 2.487 = \$4,974$$

One finds the 2.487 present value factor as the cell that reflects the 3 period column (n) and the 10% interest rate row (i) in the present value of an ordinary annuity table. The present value of an ordinary annuity table accounts for the multiple rents; therefore, one must only multiply the factor by one rent (i.e., $2,000 in this case).

Compounding defines the fact that interest accrues on previously incurred (or earned) interest as well as principal. Oftentimes, however, a debtor must make cash payments semiannually, quarterly, or monthly to its creditor, instead of annually, to satisfy the loan agreement. You can adjust the present value tables to reflect compounding that occurs more than once a year. For semiannual payments, one doubles the number of time periods (n) and halves the interest rate (i). You take the same approach for quarterly payments by quadrupling n and quartering i. For example, refer to the two Redlands time value calculations above. Assume for the moment that each transaction required semiannual compounding of interest. You compute the present value of the liabilities as follows:

Single sum of $2,000: $2,000 * .746 = $1,492 (where n = 6 and i = 5%)

Annuity of $2,000 ($1,000 paid every six months): $1,000 * 5.076 = $5,076 (where n=6 and i=5%)

Armed with this knowledge of how the time value of money affects long-term liabilities, we now examine the accounting for term bonds.

TERM BONDS

A financially viable company has numerous avenues of obtaining long-term debt financing. One prominent method is bank borrowing. Recall from Chapters 1 and 2 the notes payable that arose when Extreme Edge borrowed cash from its bank. More common than bank borrowing for major corporations is long-term debt financing obtained by issuing **term bonds**.[8] These long-term liabilities infuse cash into the business. In return for the use of the cash, the firm is contractually obligated to pay periodic interest (usually annually or semiannually) and to repay the principal when the bond matures. We now turn our attention to the accounting for term bonds.

PAR VALUE BONDS

In its most simplistic state, an entity issues bonds at par (face) value. Firms issue **par value bonds** when the **stated (legal, coupon,** or **contracted)** interest rate on the bond equals the prevailing **market (effective** or **yield)** rate of interest on the date it issues the bonds. Most issuers denominate bonds in $1,000 amounts; therefore, the firm receives $1,000 per bond upon issue in return for periodic interest payments, determined by the contracted interest rate, and the repayment of the principal ($1,000 per bond) at the end of the bond contract.

To illustrate the accounting for a par value bond, assume that Redlands issued one, $1,000, ten-year bond on January 1, 2009. The bond has a 6% interest rate and pays annual interest each December 31. The market rate of interest on January 1, 2009 was also 6%.

General Journal

Date	Accounts	Debit	Credit
1/1/09	Cash	1,000	
	Bonds payable		1,000
12/31/09	Interest expense (1,000 * .06)	60	
	Cash (1,000 * .06)		60

We verify that Redlands receives $1,000 for its promise to pay $60 annual contracted interest (an annuity) and repay $1,000 of principal (a single sum of money) at the end of ten-years by adding the present value of the two cash flows together[9]:

Present value of the single sum: $1,000 * .55839 =	$ 558.39	(n =10; i = 6%)
Present value of the annuity: $60 * 7.36009 =	+ 441.61	(n =10; i = 6%)
Cash proceeds (present value of the bond)	**$1,000.00**	

Two additional issues relate to the issuance of bonds: first, the bonds may pay interest semiannually (or quarterly) rather than annually. Second, the firm may issue the bonds at some point during the year (instead of at the beginning of the fiscal reporting period). To illustrate the first circumstance, assume the bond facts as above, except that the firm contracts to pay interest *semiannually*:

General Journal

Date	Accounts	Debit	Credit
1/1/09	Cash	1,000	
	Bonds payable		1,000
6/30/09	Interest expense (1,000 * .06 * 6/12)*	30	
	Cash (1,000 * .06 * 6/12)		30

*Note that the quote on interest rates is always the annual rate

In the second case, we assume that Redlands pays interest annually, but the firm issues the bonds on March 1, 2009. The company, consequently, will pay interest annually on February 28 of each year. The firm makes the following entries to account for the first year of the bond:

General Journal

Date	Accounts	Debit	Credit
3/1/09	Cash	1,000	
	Bonds payable		1,000
12/31/09	Interest expense (1,000 * .06 * 10/12)	50	
	Interest payable		50
2/28/10	Interest payable	50	
	Interest expense (1,000 * .06 * 2/12)	10	
	Cash (1,000 * .06 * 12/12)		60

Accountants refer to the December 31 entry as an **adjusting entry**. The firm must adjust its accounts so that the income statement reflects the correct 2009 interest expense ($50). In addition, Redlands 2009 balance sheet reports accrued interest payable ($50), as well as its obligation for the bond's principal ($1,000) on December 31.

Note that the February 28, 2010 entry records the settlement of the $50 interest payable liability (as of December 31, 2009) and the $10 of interest cost incurred from January 1 through February 28, 2010 ($1,000 * .06 * 2/12). The cash outflow for the periodic interest payment on February 28 is $60, which equates to the annual borrowing cost ($1,000 * .06 * 12/12).

Bond Discounts

The primary difficulty related to bond accounting is when the stated, legal, or contracted interest rate does not equal the market rate of interest (or yield) on the day the company issues the bond. A company must make cash payments equal to the par value of the bond (usually denominated in $1,000 amounts) multiplied by the *stated* rate of interest. The accrual-based bond *interest expense*, however, will not equal the contracted *cash payment* amount because the true cost of borrowing (interest expense) is a function of the prevailing *market* rate of interest on the date it issues the bond.

Assume for the moment that the market rate of interest was 8% for the 6% contractual interest rate bond that Redlands issued. Investors would not acquire a security yielding 6% when they could receive an 8% return on their investment elsewhere. Consequently, Redlands must lower the selling price of its 6% bond to less than $1,000, so that its cash flows yield 8%. In other words, they would sell the bond at a **discount**. Conversely, the firm would issue bonds at a **premium** (a selling price of more than $1,000 per bond) when its coupon rate exceeds the current market rate of interest. You undertake four steps when accounting for a bond sold at a discount or premium.

1. Calculate the bond issue price (its selling price or the cash received by the seller).
2. Construct a bond amortization table to eliminate the discount or premium over time.
3. Make the necessary journal entries.
4. Disclose the relevant financial statement information.

We will use the following data to illustrate accounting for bonds issued at a discount: Redlands, Inc. issued two hundred, $1,000 face value bonds on January 1, 2009. The bonds had a stated interest rate is 6%, but the market rate on that date was 8%. The firm will pay annual interest each December 31. Redlands will repay the full $200,000 principal when the bond matures in five years, on December 31, 2013.

One uses time value of money factors to compute the selling price of the bond. Specifically, related to bond accounting, this means we compute the present value of $200,000 five years into the future, plus the present value of an annuity (or equal cash payments) of $12,000 (200,000 * .06). Inasmuch as the cost of capital is 8% when the firm goes to market, one discounts the future cash flows at the 8% market rate of interest. The cash proceeds are computed as follows:

Present value of the maturity value: $200,000 * .68058 = $136,116 (n = 5; i = 8%)

Present value of the annuity: $12,000 * 3.99271 = +47,913 (n = 5; i =8%)

Cash proceeds (present value of the bonds) $184,029

Note that the cash Redlands receives ($184,029) is less than the $200,000 face or par value of the bonds. The difference between the two amounts is the **bond discount** of $15,971. Now that we know the amount of cash received, the next step in to construct a **bond amortization table**. This table helps you determine the amounts needed for the journal entries and financial statements. In reading the following table, you should realize that the goal is to eliminate (or amortize) the amount of the bond discount over the life of the bonds. You eliminate the bond discount (or premium) because the firm is contractually required to pay the face value of the bonds (i.e., $200,000 in this case) to its investors when the bond matures. Exhibit 4-5 presents the bond amortization table.

Exhibit 4-5
Bond Amortization Table for Bonds Issued at a Discount

(1) Date	(2) Cash Paid—6%	(3) Interest Expense—8%	(4) Amortized Discount	(5) Unamortized Discount	(6) Present Value of Bonds
1/1/09	-----	-----	-----	$15,971	$184,029
12/31/09	12,000	14,722	2,722	13,249	186,751
12/31/10	12,000	14,940	2,940	10,309	189,691
12/31/11	12,000	15,175	3,175	7,134	192,866
12/31/12	12,000	15,429	3,429	3,705	196,295
12/31/13	12,000	15,705	3,705	0	200,000
Totals	$60,000	$75,971	$15,971		

The bond discount amortized is the difference between the interest expense and cash paid in the table (column 3 – column 2 = column 4). The amortization of the bond discount (column 4), in turn, reduces the balance of the unamortized discount (column 5). The reduction of column 5 increases the bonds' book, or present, value (column 6).

The manager can validate that the bonds yield the *market* rate of interest that existed on January 1, 2009, the date Redlands issued the bonds. Note that 2009 interest expense is $14,722 ($184,029 * 8%), which effectively was the cost of using $184,029 of its creditors' funds. This cost equals 8% ($14,722 / $184,029). Selecting another year reinforces this concept. Consider 2012: $15,429 / $192,866 = 8%.

We now use this data to make the journal entries for the first two years.

General Journal

Date	Accounts	Debit	Credit
1/1/09	Cash	184,029	
	Discount on bonds payable	15,971	
	Bonds payable		200,000
12/31/09	Interest expense	14,722	
	Discount on bonds payable		2,722
	Cash		12,000
12/31/10	Interest expense	14,940	
	Discount on bonds payable		2,940
	Cash		12,000

Accountants refer to discount on bonds payable as a **contra-liability** because it reduces the current value of the bond from its face value to its current book value. Note that as the discount is amortized, the net book value of the bond increases, until at maturity the face value and book value are the same. Exhibit 4-6 presents the affect of the bond accounting on the financial statements over the life of the bonds:

Exhibit 4-6
Financial Statement Effects for Bonds Issued at a Discount

Income Statements

	2009	2010	2011	2012	2013
Non-operating revenues and expenses:					
Interest expense	$14,722	$14,940	$15,175	$15,429	$15,705

Balance Sheets—at December 31

	2009	2010	2011	2012	2013
Long-term liabilities:					
Bonds payable, par value	$200,000	$200,000	$200,000	$200,000	$200,000
Less: unamortized discount	(13,249)	(10,309)	(7,134)	(3,705)	0
Net book value of bonds payable	$186,751	$189,691	$192,866	$196,295	$200,000

Statements of Cash Flows

	2009	2010	2011	2012	2013
Cash flows from operating activities:					
Cash paid for bond interest	$12,000	$12,000	$12,000	$12,000	$12,000

The 2013 balance sheet presents the bonds payable immediately before Redlands settles its obligation.[10] The final journal entry for the accounting of the bonds records their payment as follows:

General Journal

Date	Accounts	Debit	Credit
12/31/13	Bonds payable	200,000.	
	Cash		200,000

As with bonds issued at par value, one must adjust the accounts at year-end if the firm sold the bonds during the year, and adjust the amortization table factors if the firm pays interest semiannually or quarterly.

BOND PREMIUMS

An equal probability exists that the firm would issue bonds when the market rate of interest was less than that stated on the bond contract. This circumstance creates a *premium* on bonds payable, rather than a discount on bonds payable. The accounting system treats the premium as an **adjunct-liability** account. The book value of the bonds at a specific point in time, therefore, reflects the face (par) value of the bonds payable *plus* the balance in the premium account. As with a discounted bond, the firm amortizes the premium over the life of the bond. When companies issue bonds at premium, the effective interest expense is *less than* the cash paid for interest.

We illustrate accounting for bond issues above par value by using the data for the Redlands bond discount problem and changing one assumption. Let us assume that the market rate of interest on January 1, 2009 was 5%, rather than 8%. Redlands would receive the following amount of cash:

Present value of the maturity value:	$200,000 * .78353 =	$156,706 (n = 5; i = 5%)
Present value of the annuity:	$12,000 * 4.32948 =	+51,954 (n = 5; i = 5%)
Cash proceeds (present value of the bonds)		**$208,660**

Exhibit 4-7 presents the amortization table for the bonds issued at a premium.

Exhibit 4-7
Bond Amortization Table for Bonds Issued at a Premium

(1) Date	(2) Cash Paid—6%	(3) Interest Expense—5%	(4) Amortized Premium	(5) Unamortized Premium	(6) Present Value of Bonds
1/1/09	-----	-----	-----	$8,660	$208,660
12/31/09	12,000	10,433	1,567	7,093	207,093
12/31/10	12,000	10,355	1,645	5,448	205,448
12/31/11	12,000	10,272	1,728	3,720	203,720
12/31/12	12,000	10,186	1,814	1,906	201,906
12/31/13	12,000	10,094	1,906	0	200,000
Totals	$60,000	$51,340	$8,660		

Notice that the premium on bonds payable (an adjunct-liability) increases the current value of the bond from its face value ($200,000) to its current book value. Exhibit 4-8 presents the impact of bonds accounted for at a premium on the financial statements:

Exhibit 4-8
Financial Statement Effects for Bonds Issued at a Premium

Income Statements

	2009	2010	2011	2012	2013
Non-operating revenues and expenses:					
Interest expense	$10,433	$10,355	$10,272	$10,186	$10,094

Balance Sheets—at December 31

	2009	2010	2011	2012	2013
Long-term liabilities:					
Bonds payable, par value	$200,000	$200,000	$200,000	$200,000	$200,000
Plus: unamortized premium	7,093	5,448	3,720	1,906	0
Net value of bonds payable	$207,093	$205,448	$203,720	$201,906	$200,000

Statements of Cash Flows

	2009	2010	2011	2012	2013
Cash flows from operating activities:					
Cash paid for bond interest	$12,000	$12,000	$12,000	$12,000	$12,000

Note that the cash paid for interest is the same for the bonds issued at a discount or a premium. This condition holds because interest payments are a function of the stated interest rate, and not the market rate of interest. The contracted or stated rate of interest was 6% for both the bonds issued at a discount and at a premium.

COST OF CAPITAL

Managers must be aware of the firm's cost of capital when making investing decisions. They would only purchase a resource, or invest in a project, if its expected benefits (earnings) exceed its cost. This last section of Chapter 4 examines how to determine the cost of capital for an entity. You will learn how to calculate the cost of debt, equity, and total financing. Knowledge of the aggregate cost of enterprise funding, known as the overall weighted average cost of capital, is especially helpful to managers when assessing investment opportunities.

DEBT COST OF CAPITAL

The **debt cost of capital** is the annual interest expense that results from borrowing money. For instance, in the example when Redlands issued bonds at a premium, the cost of borrowing was 5% of the book (or carrying) value of the bonds payable per year. Similarly, when the firm issued bonds at a discount, it effectively incurred an 8% cost of debt capital (i.e., the prevailing market rate of interest on the date of issue). Readers should always bear in mind that it is accrual expense, and not its associated cash payment, that determines the cost of debt financing.

The **weighted average cost of debt capital** (assuming no income taxes) equals total interest expense divided by total interest-bearing obligations. For example, assume that Redlands issued a five-year, 6% note payable for $100,000 and 8%, ten-year par value bonds for $300,000. Redlands weighted average cost of debt capital is computed as follows:

Interest expense / Interest-bearing liabilities
($6,000 + $24,000) / ($100,000 + $300,000)
$30,000 / $400,000 = 7.5%

Recall from the Chapter 3 discussion that interest costs shield a portion of revenues from taxation. The deductibility of interest, in turn, reduces the effective cost of debt financing. The net, or after-tax, cost of interest is interest expense multiplied by one minus the effective income tax rate. Assume that Redlands had a 40% income tax rate in the above example. The company's weighted average cost of debt capital is 4.5% computed as follows:

Net interest expense / Interest-bearing liabilities
[($6,000 + $24,000) * (1 - .40)] / ($100,000 + $300,000)
$18,000 / $400,000 = 4.5%

A manager can determine weighted average cost of debt capital from the firm's financial statements. Consider the data from Extreme Edge in Exhibit 2-1. The company reported a $10,000 interest expense on its 2008 income statement and a $120,000 notes payable on that year's balance sheet. Therefore, its pretax cost of debt capital for 2008 was 8.33% ($10,000 / $120,000).[11] The Exhibit 2-1 income statements reveal that the firm had an effective income tax rate of 40% annually. Therefore, the 2008 net cost of debt capital for Extreme Edge was 5.0% ($6,000 / $120,000 or 8.33% * .6).

Extreme Edge reported $20,000 of interest expense on its 2009 income statement and $220,000 of notes payable on its December 31, 2009 balance sheet. One can confirm the issuance of a second note in 2009 because Extreme Edge discloses $100,000 cash received from note financing in the activities section of its 2009 statement of cash flows. The firm's pretax weighted average cost of debt capital for 2009 was 9.1% ($20,000 / $220,000), and its net cost of debt capital was 5.45% ($12,000 / $220,000 or 9.1% * .6).

The pretax cost of borrowing on the 2009 note was 10%. We determine this percentage by dividing the cash proceeds of the second note ($100,000) into the $10,000 *change* in interest expense from 2008 to 2009 ($10,000 vs. $20,000). Consequently, the net cost of the 2009 note was 6% (10% * .6). The manager should note that the net cost of borrowing increased by one percentage point from 2008 to 2009 (5.0% vs. 6.0%).

Internal or external factors, or both, may explain the increased cost of debt capital. Lenders may perceive greater risk because the second note increases the firm's degree of **financial leverage** (i.e., the proportion of a firm's debt to equity financing). Alternatively, the increase in interest rate from 2008 to 2009 may have been attributable to an array of external economic factors beyond the control of Extreme Edge.

EQUITY COST OF CAPITAL

Computing the cost of debt financing is relatively straightforward because debt financing carries explicit interest rates. Such is not the case with the cost of equity financing. The manager must be able to determine the cost of equity financing implicitly.

Estimating the **cost of equity capital** is a difficult task. Managers can approximate the cost of common equity, k_s, based on its **opportunity cost**. Opportunity cost, in this case, is the rate of return investors give up by taking an equity position in the firm.[12] Conceptually, this cost equals the risk-free rate of return (k_{rf}) plus a risk premium (RP), or

$$k_s = k_{rf} + RP$$

We implement the above equation by using the interest rate on Treasury bills as a surrogate for the risk-free rate of return, and the stock's beta coefficient (b_i) as its measure of risk, yielding:

$$k_s = k_{rf} + (k_m - k_{rf})b_i$$

Where:

k_m = expected return on the overall equity market.

Managers must understand the concept of the **beta coefficient** or **beta** or **b** to appreciate the equation presented above.[13] In turn, he or she must understand that beta is a market-derived metric. Equity markets classify risk into two components: systematic and unsystematic risk. Owners eliminate a substantial portion of their risk by diversifying their investments. That strategy eliminates much of the risk inherent in investing in a single asset, or a small group of resources. Investors call the type of risk that one can eliminate through diversification as **unsystematic risk** or **diversifiable risk**.

Firm-specific events cause unsystematic risk. Examples include the success (or failure) of business operations, product introductions, and market penetrations. Some risk, referred to as **systematic** or **market risk**, cannot be eliminated through diversification. Systematic risk occurs because certain events affect the value of all firms. Examples of market risk include (or exclude) war, inflation, recession, and high interest rates.

The extent to which an entity's share price moves in relation to the overall market movement is its beta, which analysts measure by the firm's beta coefficient.[14] The overall market has a beta coefficient of 1.0. This unity exists because the market's reaction to an event is, by definition, its change based on a specific event. Individual firm's share prices; however, do not move in lockstep with the rate of change that occurs in the overall market. Some firms do not exhibit as much volatility to systematic risk as the overall market, while the magnitude of price change to such events for other firms exceeds that of the market as a whole. Less reactive firms have betas that range from zero to slightly less than 1.0. Companies whose volatility exceeds that of the market have betas of greater than 1.0.

The cost of equity equation enables the manager to estimate the firm's cost of equity capital. Assume for the moment that Extreme Edge had a beta of 1.2, Treasury bills (a risk-free investment) were yielding a 2.4% return on investment, and the rate of return in the stock market has averaged 7%. Extreme Edge's cost of equity capital is as follows:

$$k_s = k_{rf} + (k_m - k_{rf})b_i$$
$$7.9\% = 2.4\% + (7.0\% - 2.4\%) * 1.2$$

WEIGHTED AVERAGE COST OF CAPITAL

A manager combines the cost of debt financing with that of equity financing to determine the firms **weighted average cost of capital** (WACC). The equation is as follows:

WACC = (% of debt) (net cost of debt) + (% of common stock) (cost of common equity)

or

$$WACC = w_d k_d (1-T) + w_s k_s$$

Where:

w = weight of capital component [calculated as the value of the capital component (debt or equity)/ value of all capital components added together]

$_d$ = debt

$_s$ = common stock equity

k_d = weighted interest rate on the firm's debt

T = marginal income tax rate

k_s = cost of common stock equity

A manager can use the above weighted average cost of capital equation to compute the firm's WACC. For example, excerpted 2009 financial statement data for Extreme Edge (Exhibit 2-1) are as follows:

Income Statement Excerpts

Interest (financial) expense	$20,000
Income tax rate	40%

Balance Sheet Excerpts

Long-term liabilities:

Notes payable	$220,000

Shareholders' Equity

Common stock	80,000
Additional paid-in-capital	420,000
Total contributed capital	
Retained Earnings	44,000
Total shareholders' equity	544,000

In addition, we assume that the same market data: a beta of 1.2, Treasury bills yielding 2.4%, and an average stock market return of 7%.

Extreme Edge's 2009 WACC is as follows:

$$WACC = w_d k_d (1-T) + w_s k_s$$
$$WACC = (.288 * .091 * .60) + (.712 * .079)$$
$$WACC = .0157 + .0562$$
$$WACC = .0719$$
$$WACC = 7.19\%$$

Based on Extreme Edge's weighted average cost of capital, the manager would not invest in an asset or project unless it produced a return on investment of at least 7.19%.

Summary

Chapter 4 presented the accounting processes for equity and debt financing, thereby examining the journal transactions and the effect on financial statement disclosures. One acquires resources, or invests in projects, when the expected return on investment exceeds the cost of capital.

Equity financing consists of three major categories: contributed capital, retained earnings, and treasury stock. Contributed capital and retained earnings expand firm capital via external and internal funding, respectively. Treasury stock transactions contract equity financing by acquiring issued shares of stock in the marketplace. Such transactions reduce cash and the number of outstanding shares.

The time value of money concept affects accounting for long-term debt financing. This chapter discussed why a dollar today is worth more than a dollar in the future, and how the accounting system adjusts for the timing disparities of cash receipts and cash payments. The reader also learned that fluctuating interest rates influence accrual-based interest expense charges, and that discount and premium amortization schedules enable the manager to measure the effective cost of borrowing and its impact on financial statement disclosures.

This chapter concluded with equations that measured the cost of capital for debt and equity, as well as the overall cost of entity financing. Knowledge of weighted average cost of capital enables managers to make sound investment decisions. One invests only when the expected return on investment equals or exceeds the cost of capital.

Key Terms

Additional paid-in-capital on treasury stock transactions
Additional paid-in-capital in excess of par value
Adjunct-liability
Adjusting entry
Annuity
Authorized shares
Beta coefficient (beta or b)
Bond amortization table
Bond discount
Capital gain
Common stock (common shares)
Compounding
Contra-liability
Cost of equity capital
Debt cost of capital
Discount
Dividend
Dividend declaration date
Dividend payment date
Financial leverage
Issued shares
Market rate of interest (effective interest rate or yield)
Opportunity cost
Outstanding shares
Par value (stated value)
Par value bonds
Preferred stock (preferred shares)
Premium
Present value
Present value table
Present value table factor
Rents
Single (lump) sum of money
Stated rate of interest (legal, coupon, or contracted interest rate)
Systematic risk (market risk)
Term bonds
Time value of money
Treasury shares

Unsystematic risk (diversifiable risk)
Weighted average cost of capital
Weighted average cost of debt capital

Assignments

Accounting Concepts Crossword

Across

[1] The discount on bonds payable is a ___-___ account because it reduces the current value of the bond from its face value to its current book value.

[2] Issued stock that a firm buys for retirement or resale.

[3] All corporations issue this type of stock.

[4] The amount by which the market price of a bond is lower than its principal amount due at maturity.

[5] The minimum selling price of a share of stock when the firm issues it.

Down

[1] Distributions of the earnings of a corporation to its owners.

[2] An issue of bonds that repay principal upon maturity.

[3] A class of stock that typically has dividend and liquidation preferences.

[4] Equal cash payments equally spaced.

[5] Bonds issued when the market rate of interest is less than that stated on the bond contract.

Discussion Items

What Would Your Accountant Say?

Your company is considering raising capital for a new expansion project and the president has asked you to give a presentation to the board of directors that examines the risks and benefits of funding the project with debt versus equity financing. What would your accountant say?

Theory vs. Practice

As discussed in the chapter, preferred stock offers an investor certain preferences over common stock in relation to dividends and liquidation value. In theory, these preferences should make preferred shares more attractive to potential investors than common stock. In practice, however, majorities of companies do not issue preferred stock, and most investors seem to favor putting their investment dollars into common shares. Discuss some of the reasons a company might not issue preferred stock, and why most investors choose common over preferred.

Problems

Problem 4-1

MI Air, Inc. engages in the following *common* stock transactions in 2010 for its $1 par value common stock. The firm earned $200 of net income during 2010, its first year of business.

1. January 1—Issued 200 shares to an investor for $8 per share.
2. January 1—Issued 100 shares to its attorney/CPA as compensation for establishing the company. (Treat the value of the shares as an organizational expense.)
3. December 1—Purchased 40 of the shares sold to the investor for $10 per share, and placed them in the corporate treasury.
4. December 10—Issued 75 shares to another investor at $9 per share in order to secure additional financing for the firm.
5. December 12—Issued 30 of the treasury shares when the market price was $11 per share.
6. December 15—Declared a $.20 per share dividend.
7. December 31—Paid the dividend declared on December 15.

Requirements: (Use T-accounts as necessary to track account balances)
   a. Journalize the above transactions.

b. Present the effects of the stock transactions on MI Air's 2010 income statement, and report stockholders' equity on the company's December 31, 2010 balance sheet.

Problem 4-2

Blacklands, Inc. issues 300 $1,000 bonds on May 1, 2009. The bonds stated interest rate is 8%, but the market rate on that date is 6%. The firm will pay interest semiannually on each October 31 and April 30. Blacklands will repay the full $300,000 principal when the bonds mature on April 30, 2014.

Required:

a. Calculate the bond issue price (its selling price) on May 1, 2009.
b. Construct a bond amortization table on Excel. Use the following partial table as your template:

Date	Cash Paid	Interest Expense	Amortized Disc./ Premium	Unamortized Disc./ Premium	Present Value of Bonds
5/1/09					
10/31/09					
4/30/10					
10/31/10					

c. Make the necessary journal entries through December 31, 2009. (Include the adjusting entry on December 31, 2009 by pro-rating the April 30, 2010 amortization table values.)
d. Disclose the relevant financial statement information for 2009 (income statement, balance sheet, and statement of cash flows).

Problem 4-3

Subtle Edge, Inc. presents the following excerpts from its December 31, 2010 balance sheet:

Current Liabilities:
Notes payable, 8% $200,000
Long-term Liabilities:
Bonds payable, 10%   1,000,000
Shareholders' Equity
Common stock, par   50,000
Additional paid-in-capital, common stock _350,000_
   Total contributed capital   400,000
Retained earnings   _250,000_
   Total shareholders' equity $650,000

The accounting department also conveys the following information:

Risk-free rate of return—3%
Average market rate of return—7.5%
Beta—.90
Income tax rate of 30%

Required:

Compute Subtle Edge's net cost of debt, equity, and overall cost of capital.

Case 4-1

Lightpoint, Inc. is a computer software company that seeks external financing in order to support its growth initiatives. As a relatively new firm, Lightpoint has generated scant profits and produced meager cash flows from operations to date. Sharon Light, the firm's founder and CEO, charged her Chief Financial Officer (CFO), Richard McManus, with securing debt financing that the firm can service with its income level and cash flows. Working with Lightpoint's investment banker (IB), McManus thought he found a potential solution to the problem. McManus agreed with the IB that the concept of floating *zero-percent* or *deep-discount* bonds deserved serious consideration.

Befitting its name, zero-percent bonds do not pay periodic interest, unlike conventional term bonds. Zero-percent bonds operate in the following manner:

- The firm receives an amount of cash upon issue that equals the present value of the amount it must repay upon maturity.
- It does not pay interest periodically to the bondholders in such an arrangement.
- The current market rate of interest determines the difference between the future value of money and its present value. (This difference is the amount of the bond discount, or the time value of money.)

Zero-percent bonds usually increase the borrower's cost of financing because the cash payments are loaded at the back-end of the bond contract. Investors demand a higher return on their investment for undertaking a greater degree of risk in such arrangements. Issuers structure deep discount bonds (other than zero-percent bonds) in a manner similar to zero-percent bonds, except the firm makes relatively small periodic interest payments on the par value of the bonds. For example, a firm may issue bonds that pay 1% interest when the effective rate of interest is 5% on the deeply discounted bonds. CFO McManus identified three financing avenues by which Lightpoint could raise $200 million in capital on January 1, 2009. The firm could float bonds that mature on December 31, 2018 in one of three ways:

1. Conventional 4% par value, term bonds that pay interest annually interest on December 31.
2. Zero-percent term bonds (effectively yielding 6% interest).
3. Deeply discounted 1% term bonds (effectively yielding 5% interest and paying 1% interest each December 31).

The investment bank informs McManus that it can place the bonds with a private investor. Such a placement means that Lightpoint will be able to forego the time and expense normally associated with a public bond offering. The upshot of the private placement is that Lightpoint will not incur any material transaction costs.In considering the firm's financing alternatives, McManus estimated that Lightpoint would generate a little over $3 million annually in excess liquidity in the near term. That surplus cash could be used to pay periodic bond financing charges if necessary. As McManus embarks on *running the numbers* for the alternatives, he gathers the following time value of money factors for ten time periods:

	4%	5%	6%
Future value of 1 (lump sum)	1.48024	1.62889	1.79085
Present value of 1 (lump sum)	.67556	.61391	.55839
Future value of an annuity	12.00611	12.57789	13.18079
Present value of an annuity	8.11090	7.72173	7.36009

One final factor that McManus considers is that the firm's lack of profitability has mitigated its income tax exposure. Consequently, income taxes will not affect his calculations or recommendation.

Required:

Cast yourself in the role of Richard McManus. Make a financing recommendation to Sharon Light in a memo. Be sure to discuss the financial implications of each alternative on the income statements, balance sheets, and statement of cash flows for 2009 and 2010 in your memo. You must attach an Excel spreadsheet(s) that contains calculations for the full ten years under each financing arrangement in order to support your financial statement implications for the next two years and your recommendation contained in the memo.

Endnotes

1. As one might infer from the first and second chapters of this text, accounting for the fees and donations of not-for-profit entities is less detailed than accounting for equity infusions into corporations. Governments statutorily mandate non-reciprocal wealth transfers, while health and welfare organizations secure voluntary contributions. Neither of these activities results in the complex accounting issues of corporate finance.

2. Some firms refer to preferred shares as Class A or Class 1 stock; and they call common shares Class B or Class 2 stock.

3. Corporations convert all assets into cash when they liquidate. Subsequently, and to the extent that funds permit, the firm settles creditor claims, and then returns investments to the shareholders. As a practical matter, most firms that liquidate are bankrupt and common shareholders do not receive a return of their investment.

4. Other types of dividends, most notably stock dividends, exist besides cash dividends. The accounting for these types of dividends exceeds the scope of this text.

5. Paying a dividend on treasury stock is analogous to the firm taking money out of its left pocket and placing it the right one.

6. The accounting system does not equate current liabilities to their present value because the time difference between the balance sheet date and the settlement date is immaterial.

7. Firms always quote interest rates in annual terms.

8. Alternative to term bonds exist, such as serial bonds. This text ignores these less prominent types of corporate finance because of the greater accounting and mathematical complexities inherent in them.

9. We extend present value factors two additional decimal places to insure greater precision. We also do this when computing discounted and premium bonds later in the chapter.

10. Redlands could reclassify its bonds payable as a current liability at the end of 2008 because it will settle the obligation within one year.

11. This assumes that the firm issued the note at the beginning of 2008.

12. Chapter 5 explores the concept of opportunity costs in greater detail.

13. This discussion excerpts features of the efficient market hypothesis (EMH) and capital asset pricing model (CAPM). We do so in order to create an understanding of the cost of equity financing. The authors refer the reader to a comprehensive text on financial management or equity investing in order to appreciate the importance of EMH and CAPM.

14. Virtually all reputable financial sources list corporate betas.

Chapter 5

Cost Considerations

CHAPTER LEARNING OBJECTIVES

Upon completion of this chapter, readers should be able to:
- ➤ Interpret the numerous meanings and dimensions of the concept of cost.
- ➤ Differentiate between the effects of product and period costs on financial disclosures.
- ➤ Understand how variable-cost income statements align managerial performance with corporate objectives.
- ➤ Establish standard product costs and apply factory overhead to them.
- ➤ Account for direct materials, direct labor, and factory overhead in a job-order-costing environment.
- ➤ Improve product costing and pricing decisions with activity-based-costing.

Managers secure financing, make investments, and conduct operations in order to meet organizational goals. Paramount among the objectives is wealth creation by profit-seeking firms and societal service by not-for-profit entities. Ultimately, all managers seek to allocate their scarce resources efficiently, regardless of the specific decision objective. An efficient accounting system, therefore, must provide managers with relevant and reliable operating data, in addition to producing periodic financial statements.

Timely accounting data enables managers to conduct business operations. This financial information is essential to determining product cost, establishing sales prices, and selecting markets. Chapter 5 begins to explore the relationship between operating accounting information and managerial decisions. The next two chapters of the text continue this process. This chapter specifically examines the numerous dimensions that compose the concept of cost, how the accounting system measures cost, and the role of cost data in managerial decision processes.

COST FACTORS

The net benefit produced by a managerial decision is the difference between the resources that a course of action generates and the investment base it consumes. One can regard each managerial action as a decision-specific income statement: revenue minus expenses equals net income. Recognizing revenue as earned is a straightforward endeavor—product price multiplied by quantity sold. Matching expenses to revenue, however, is a more difficult task because the associated expenses stem from underlying costs. The concept of cost, in turn, has multiple meanings. The multi-faceted perspective of cost challenges managers to account for costs appropriately and accurately. This requires managers to interpret and apply the specific nuances of the generic notion of cost to specific circumstances in order to make good decisions.

A **cost** is what an entity gives up to obtain something of value. Accountants define cost as "the sacrifice incurred in economic activities—that which is given up or foregone to consume, to save, to exchange, to produce, and so forth."[1] In most instances, the sacrifice is either a cash payment or a promise to pay cash in the future. Viewed from a manager's perspective, a cost is what a company incurs to acquire the economic resources (assets) needed to conduct business. The firm uses those assets to sell goods and provide services, thereby earning income and generating cash. Successful firms create wealth by generating more cash from their resources than they pay out to acquire them.[2]

CAPITAL AND REVENUE EXPENDITURES

As noted from our Chapter 1 and 2 discussions, you subtract specific amounts of costs from revenues in order to determine income for a particular reporting period. An **expense**, therefore, is that portion of the cost of the economic resource (or asset) consumed within a specific reporting period. Sometimes current revenue generation exhausts the entire cost, in which case a company reports the total monetary amount of the sacrifice as an expense. Managers refer to these costs as **revenue expenditures**. On the other hand, certain economic sacrifices produce revenues in future reporting periods as well as present ones; therefore, an entity allocates such costs as expenses over multiple reporting periods. A company initially reports such **capital (or asset) expenditures** on its balance sheet and apportions those costs as expenses to the applicable reporting periods.

Consider two costs in order to grasp the difference between revenue and capital expenditures. Extreme Edge (our fictitious corporate exemplar) classifies its administrative costs as revenue expenditures because those economic sacrifices only contribute to the current reporting period's revenue. On the other hand, the firm initially classifies purchased inventory as a capital expenditure (i.e., an asset reported on the balance sheet). The Internet merchant's cost of goods sold expense (an expense on the income statement) depends on the amount of inventory the company sells in a reporting period. If, for example, Extreme Edge did not sell any products in a given reporting period, it would not report any of its inventoried cost (the capital expenditure) as an expense.[3]

Managerial strategies affect revenue and capital expenditures. Extreme Edge demonstrates how such corporate decisions influence cost disclosure. The company does not own any land or buildings, choosing to rent space instead. Extreme Edge's rental cost helps the e-tailer earn revenues during each reporting period, but not in any future ones. The rent, therefore, is revenue expenditure, or more simply rent expense. Alternatively, the company purchased equipment to assist in controlling inventory and filling orders from customers. The equipment is a long-term investment that supports business operations. It is, in other words, a capital expenditure.

Extreme Edge discloses rent expense and depreciation expense (for the equipment) as part of its selling and administrative expenses (operating expenses) on its income statement in the current reporting period. The firm reports the remaining equipment cost as a fixed asset on its balance sheet, which we refer to as the net (book or carrying) value. None of the rental expenditure appears on the statement of financial position, because the rent cannot contribute to Extreme Edge's earnings in future reporting periods. The company, therefore, completely charges the total cost of rent against revenues on the current period's income statement.[4]

The decision to classify a cost as either a capital or revenue expenditure is not as simple as you might conclude from the Extreme Edge example. Practical considerations sometimes outweigh theoretical correctness when classifying costs. Research and development (R&D) costs illustrate the reporting dilemma. Companies incur R&D costs in an attempt to create marketable products. Firms anticipate that such expenditures will produce revenues well into the future. In many industries, especially high-tech ones, these costs are critical in creating wealth. GAAP, however, requires that companies report these costs as revenue expenditures.[5] The FASB created this rule because the success (i.e., value or payoff) of individual R&D projects is uncertain. In other words, companies classify these costs as revenue expenditures rather than as capital ones.[6]

GAAP's stance on R&D costs conservatively measures pretax income because a company immediately subtracts product creation-related development expenditures from revenues in the current reporting period.[7] Treatment of research and development cost is not unique. Marketing costs offer another notable example of financial disclosure conservatism. As a direct marketing concern, Extreme Edge advertises to attract customers. The future benefits derived from advertisements are irrelevant from a financial reporting perspective because GAAP requires expensing these costs immediately. A manager, however, must consider future earnings potential when evaluating these types of revenue expenditures. The quantity, and more importantly, the quality of research, development, and marketing costs significantly affect future profit and cash flow, despite financial reporting treatment to the contrary.

PRODUCT AND PERIOD COSTS

The differentiation of revenue and capital expenditures helps the manager distinguish between product and period costs. **Product costs** are inventory-related expenditures. The sale of inventoried items (assets) produces revenues, and creates costs of goods sold (an expense) when the firm recognizes those revenues. **Period costs**, on the other hand, consist of non-inventoried costs consumed in the current period. The income statement reports the entire amount of these latter cost types as expenses in the period incurred. In the terminology of the previous section, virtually all period costs are revenue expenditures. This means that period costs reduce income in the current reporting period, regardless of the level of sales recognized. Conversely, a cause and effect relationship exists between revenues and product costs (i.e., cost of goods sold directly results from the quantity of products sold in any given period).[8] As noted earlier in this chapter, cost of goods sold is zero if the firm does not recognize any revenues in the period.

Some costs are either period or product costs, depending on the circumstances. To understand what causes alternative costing for such items, one must differentiate between merchandising and manufacturing concerns. A *merchant* acquires goods in a completed state from a manufacturer or wholesaler and markets them to end-use consumers. A *manufacturer*, on the other hand, converts raw materials into completed products and then sells the finished goods to its customers. The purchase price of inventory is a retailer's product cost. A manufacturer's product cost, on the other hand, includes raw materials, partially completed goods (also known as work-in-process or WIP), and finished goods inventory. This transformative process complicates the accounting for a manufacturer's product costs.

Exhibit 5-1 contrasts inventory-related costs for merchandising and manufacturing concerns.

Exhibit 5-1

Product Costing - Inventory

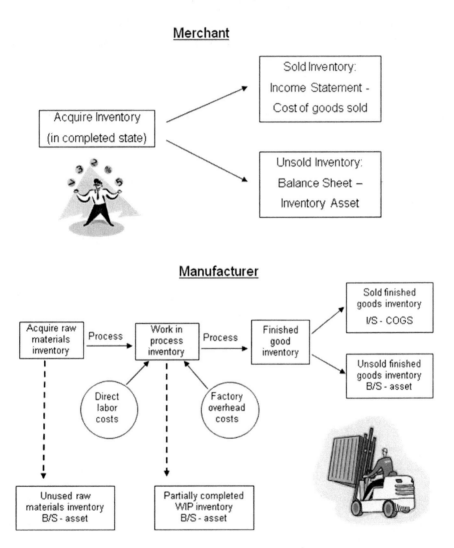

A manufacturer needs direct labor, indirect labor, and miscellaneous other materials to convert direct materials into finished goods. The manufacturer also incurs taxes and consumes a portion of its equipment and manufacturing facilities (through depreciation) to produce finished products. The costs of these inputs and processes attach to the direct materials' cost, and taken together, they become inventory costs for a manufacturer (an asset). Consequently, wages, utilities, and depreciation are product costs if manufacturers incur them in producing finished goods. The inventoried costs for manufacturing concerns, therefore, consist of raw materials, direct labor used to make goods, and manufacturing overhead costs (the indirect costs of production). The income statement reports inventoried items as cost of goods sold expense when the firm *sells* products. The firm's balance sheet discloses the cost of the *unsold* manufactured items as inventory assets.

Assume for the moment that Extreme Edge manufactured products, rather than purchasing completed inventory from vendors. The company would have to compute the cost of each product it manufactured, based on direct material, direct labor, and overhead costs—a far more complex accounting task than recording the purchases of completed goods from its vendors. Extreme Edge would disclose raw materials, work in process, and finished goods inventories on its balance sheet in this circumstance.[9] It would match the cost of completed inventory (finished goods) against revenues on its income statement when Extreme Edge sells its products.

Exhibit 5-2 summarizes the issues affecting product and period costs for merchants and manufacturers.

Exhibit 5-2
Inventory-Related Accounts
Merchants and Manufacturers

Item	Merchant	Manufacturer
Inventory type	One type: unsold finished goods	Three types: raw materials, work in process, and unsold finished goods
Measurement of inventory as a product cost	Purchase price	Direct materials, direct labor, and factory overhead (e.g., indirect raw materials, indirect labor, depreciation, rent, utilities, property taxes, and so forth)
Cost of goods sold expense	Historical cost of inventory items sold in a reporting period	Historical cost of *finished goods* sold in a period
Period costs	All salaries, rent, depreciation, utilities, etc.	Salaries, rent, depreciation, utilities, etc., related to *selling* the inventory (but not in making it)

The upper portion of the income statement for both the merchant and manufacturer is identical: sales revenues − cost of goods sold = gross profit (or gross margin). Cost of goods sold differs between the two business types;

however, as one might infer from the disclosures in Exhibit 5-2. Exhibit 5-3 presents the cost of goods sold section for a merchandising concern and a manufacturing one:

Exhibit 5-3
Cost of Goods Sold Section (Cost of Sales)
Merchants and Manufacturers

Merchant	Manufacturer
Beginning inventory (obtained from suppliers)	Beginning inventory of *finished* goods
+ Purchases of inventory (obtained from suppliers)	+ Cost of goods manufactured
= Goods (inventory) available for sale	Finished goods (inventory) available for sale
- Beginning inventory (obtained from suppliers)	- Ending inventory of *finished* goods
Cost of goods sold (or cost of sales)	Cost of goods sold (or cost of sales)

Note from Exhibit 5-3 that a manufacturer reports **cost of goods manufactured** (the second line) in its cost of goods sold section. That term captures the conversion process inherent in manufacturing: raw materials (inventory) → finished (manufactured) goods (inventory). The cost accountant, therefore, must compute the cost of goods manufactured (COGM), because finished goods inventory includes the cost of all direct materials, direct labor, and factory overhead incurred in the manufacturing process. Conversely, a merchant does not have to *calculate* its purchases. A retailer's purchases account merely reflects the acquisition cost of merchandise acquired from suppliers multiplied by the quantity acquired.

Exhibit 5-4 presents the process for calculating cost of goods manufactured:

Exhibit 5-4
Cost of Goods Manufactured Statement
(A Portion of a Manufacturer's Cost of Goods Sold Section)

Beginning raw materials inventory
+Purchases of raw materials
Raw materials available for use
- Ending raw materials inventory
Raw materials used
+ Direct labor incurred

+ Factory overhead

Total manufacturing costs

+ Beginning work in process inventory

- Ending work in process inventory

Cost of goods manufactured (for the reporting period)

Note from Exhibit 5-4 that the accounting system must measure the amount of *raw materials used* in the current reporting period.[10] The upper portion of the COGM statement (i.e., its first five lines) derives the raw materials used to make inventoried products. The *raw materials used* account, couples the materials consumed in the manufacturing process with labor and overhead costs to determine total manufacturing costs for a reporting period. The final portion of the COGM statement adjusts total manufacturing costs for partially completed goods. The statement must make this adjustment because the firm wishes to sell finished goods (not its inventories of raw materials or work in process).

COST BEHAVIOR AND ALIGNMENT

Accountants can also dichotomize costs into fixed and variable components. A **fixed cost** remains constant in total dollar amount, regardless of activity level (such as units sold or produced).[11] Viewed from a per unit perspective, however, the amount of a fixed cost decreases as activity increases because there are more units of production (or sales) to absorb the fixed cost. Conversely, a **variable cost** remains constant in monetary amount on a *per unit* basis, regardless of activity. Total variable costs increase in lockstep with an increase in activity and vice-versa as activity declines.[12] Managers can use cost behavior information in order to gain financial insights and make better decisions. For example, we now explore how the firm can use its knowledge of cost behavior to align specific actions with overall corporate objectives.[13]

External financial statements must comply with generally accepted accounting principles. GAAP-based disclosures, however, do not always provide good information for internal decisions as our discussion on R&D demonstrated. Strict adherence to GAAP, in fact, can sometimes diminish wealth rather than create it. A good accounting system, therefore, must be flexible enough to comply with GAAP for external reporting purposes, while at the same time meeting internal management needs. For example, an adaptable accounting system allows managers to alter the GAAP-mandated income statement to provide a more relevant measure of operating performance. We combine our knowledge of cost behavior with information about product and period costs to demonstrate this process.

GAAP requires allocating all product costs, both fixed and variable, to the income statement for the portion of inventory sold in the reporting period, and to the balance sheet for the unsold amount. Accountants commonly refer to this treatment as **absorption costing**. This accounting treatment yields a **full-cost (absorption-cost) income statement**. As with any fixed cost, however, fixed *product* costs are constant in total; they do not vary with productivity levels. (e.g., Property taxes incurred on factory buildings are stable, regardless of the level of production within the factory.) A **variable-cost income statement** treats *fixed* product costs as a period cost. Under **variable costing**, the firm matches the entire amount of fixed product costs against current revenues, regardless of sales level. An entity only accounts for the *variable* portion of manufacturing costs as a product cost under the variable costing approach. Proponents of variable costing argue that treating manufacturing costs based on behavior, rather than the basis of a GAAP classification (cost of goods sold), more accurately reflects economic reality and leads to better managerial decisions.

The reader should bear in mind two critical factors regarding manufacturing cost accounting. First, GAAP does not allow a firm to report earnings based on a variable-cost income statement for external disclosure purposes (i.e., published financial statements). Second, and perhaps more importantly, variable cost income statements can be an important tool for effectively managing the firm and aligning goals throughout the organization. We demonstrate the value of variable costing for managerial decisions in the following example.

Assume that Redlands, Inc. manufactures and sells 10 units of finished goods in 2010. Furthermore, it does not carry any inventory. We summarize the data as follows:

Sales	10 units @ $20
Variable product costs	$5 per unit
Fixed product costs	$60
Beginning inventory	0 units
Ending inventory	0 units

Redlands would report the same amount of earnings under full- and variable-costing as the following incomes statements demonstrate:

Full (Absorption) Costing		Variable Costing	
Sales revenues ($20 * 10 units)	$200	Sales revenues ($20 * 10 units)	$200
COGS (Variable—$5 * 10 units)	50	Variable manufacturing exp. ($5 *10)	50
COGS (Fixed—$60)	<u>60</u>	Fixed manufacturing expense	<u>60</u>
Gross profit	$ 90	Gross profit[14]	$ 90

Now use the same data as above, except assume that Redlands produces 15 units and reports the five unsold units in ending inventory. The alternative data are as follows:

Sales	10 units @ $20
Variable product costs	$5 per unit
Fixed product costs	$60
Beginning inventory	0 units
Ending inventory	5 units

The following income statements demonstrate that absorption costing and variable costing yield different amounts of net income:

Absorption Costing		Variable Costing	
Sales Revenues ($20 * 10 units)	$200	Sales revenues ($20 * 10 units)	$200
COGS (Variable—$5 * 10 units)	50	Variable manufacturing exp. ($5 *10)	50
COGS (Fixed—$60 * 2/3)	<u>40</u>	Fixed manufacturing expense	<u>60</u>
Gross profit	$110	Gross profit	$90

Absorption costing produces a higher gross profit than variable costing ($110 vs. $90) when ending inventory exceeds beginning inventory. This result occurs because under the GAAP-approved absorption approach, the firm capitalizes $20 of its fixed product costs (i.e., one third of the $60 total fixed product cost). Variable costing, on the other hand, expenses the full $60 of fixed manufacturing costs. Viewed from a balance sheet perspective, the firm would disclose the alternative amounts for its five unsold units of inventory as $45 under absorption costing and $25 for variable costing. The following table presents the specific calculations and balance sheet disclosures at December 31, 2010:

Absorption Costing		Variable Costing	
Variable cost of inventory (5 * $5)	$25	Variable cost of inventory (5 * $5)	$25
Fixed cost of inventory ($60 * 1/3)	20	Fixed cost of inventory	0
Ending inventory, cost of 5 units	$45	Ending inventory, cost of 5 units	$25

Assume for the moment that Redlands operates under the alternative assumption (i.e., it produces 15 units and sells 10 of them). Furthermore, the firm pays its departmental manager a 10% bonus on gross profit. Measuring gross profit on an absorption basis clearly creates the incentive for the manager to overproduce relative to the sales level. In doing so, the manager can shift a portion of fixed product costs from the income statement to the balance sheet. This strategy maximizes the manager's bonus, but is detrimental to the corporate objective of minimizing the holding cost of inventory. Such inequity between production and sales levels is contrary to sound inventory management and not in the best interest of the firm. Consequently, Redlands (and all other entities) should use a variable cost income statement to determine managerial bonuses. This arrangement would add the greatest value to the firm inasmuch as it rewards efficiency instead of needless production.

COST CONTROL

Corporate executives must make certain economic sacrifices at specific times in order to sustain operations. Sometimes, however, they have greater flexibility with regard to the timing and amount of these sacrifices. We define this latter category as **controllable costs**, as opposed to the former ones, which are the **uncontrollable costs** required for business operations. Inventory and advertising costs for Extreme Edge illustrate the difference. The firm must acquire and pay for its inventory in a timely manner. Vendors would not deal with the company otherwise, and a lack of products would force the company out of business. Consequently, Extreme Edge's inventory (and related cost of goods sold) is an uncontrollable cost.[15] Alternatively, management decides how much to spend to promote the company and its products. This cost, therefore, is one that management controls (a controllable cost).

Managerial changes to controllable costs affect financial statement disclosures. Managers who decrease, postpone, or eliminate controllable costs can dramatically increase corporate earnings, but they do so at the risk of hamstringing future performance. For example, assume that Extreme Edge reduced its promotional costs. This tactic would increase short-run profitability by lowering advertising expense.

The lack of brand recognition, however, could erode the firm's ability to create wealth in the long-term.

Controllable costs are also known as **discretionary costs**. Befitting this moniker, managers must determine the optimal amount of controlled spending in order to produce short-term profitability *and* ensure long-term wealth creation. The accounting system assists managers in this endeavor by measuring the amount spent on controllable costs. More importantly, accountants should help managers forecast the financial implications of alternative discretionary spending behavior.

Cost Composition

Companies usually sell multiple products or provide more than one service to its customers. This **product mix** yields a cost structure that affects overall corporate income. Managers must realize that changes in the overall product mix, or the cost composition of specific products, changes profitability. An informative accounting system enables managers to model different product mixes and pricing strategies to gauge their effects on cost composition and resulting profits. In essence, the accounting system should provide the pertinent financial data to managers who ask, "What are the financial implications of a change in current product mix, sales price, cost composition, or markets?"

Consider the activity of Extreme Edge. It buys merchandise from an array of vendors. The firm marks up the acquisition cost of its goods to establish retail prices. In all likelihood, the percentage product markup will differ among the different types of merchandise. Furthermore, marketing strategies often dictate pricing. For example, the e-tailer might sell some goods at, near, or even below cost to increase sales volume and entice shoppers to their Web site. In addition, the company probably increases selling prices for high demand products and reduces them for slow-moving merchandise.

An entity's **gross profit margin** (i.e., its gross profit divided by sales revenues), is a function of average sales price and average cost of goods sold for a given reporting period. Gross profit margins remain constant over multiple reporting periods only to the extent that the entity's pricing strategies and sales mix remain constant. If they differ, then cost of goods sold and gross profit change as a percentage of sales revenue. These changes affect reported earnings.

ALTERNATIVE COSTS

Every time an entity invests in a particular asset, it foregoes the opportunity to use those funds to acquire another resource. Accounting systems, however, measure only transacted costs; they do not capture the costs that *did not* occur. Managers must always consider the potential benefits given up, called **opportunity costs**, when evaluating performance. In addition to analyzing financial statements for what occurred, the manager should also consider what could have resulted if management had invested differently.[16] Only then can one determine if management made the best decisions to maximize entity wealth. Analyzing opportunity costs is a hypothetical exercise. Companies cannot reverse the resource decisions that produced income statement expenses and balance sheet assets. Managers, however, can use accounting data to project possible outcomes if the company had pursued alternative investment strategies. This exercise can improve managerial acumen and result in better decisions in the future.

Transacted costs are **sunk costs**. Managers must review the relative success of sunk costs (and assess the opportunities foregone) in order to forecast future performance. Managers with a proven record of creating wealth from transacted costs have reason to feel confident that future resource investments will add value to the firm. Conversely, evidence of inefficient sunk costs should spur managers (as well as their boards and shareholders) to critically evaluate and possibly change their decision-making processes. One attribute of the accounting system is that it provides a scorecard of managerial performance. We will learn how to analyze managerial performance and give it contextual meaning in a later chapter of this text.

PRODUCT COSTING SYSTEMS

As noted earlier in this chapter, product costing for a manufacturer is more complicated than that of a retailer or service organization. A manufacturing enterprise can account for its products' cost in one of two primary ways: a job order costing system or a process costing system. Firms use **process costing** when they produce numerous units of equivalent quality, such as gallons of gasoline or concrete construction blocks. The process is highly standardized and raw materials move through numerous stages or departments in order to produce the finished product. Under **job-order costing**, the entity produces similar, but not identical, products. A publisher, for example, could produce books, booklets, newspapers, flyers, and banners. The substance of process and job order costing is the same: to determine the cost of a manufactured product. The multiple divisions inherent in process costing complicate its accounting; therefore, we use job order costing to demonstrate the essence of product costing.

The manufacturer adds direct labor and factory overhead costs to raw materials in order to produce finished goods, regardless of whether it uses a process or job order costing system. Direct materials and direct labor costs compose the primary manufacturing costs, and accountants refer to these two costs as **prime costs**. They define direct labor and factory overhead as **conversion costs**, or the cost of transforming raw materials into finished goods. The critical factor in determining a product's cost is the proper allocation of overhead cost. We now turn our attention to the technique that enables the entity to add factory overhead costs to its prime costs in order to calculate the total cost of a manufactured product.

APPLIED FACTORY OVERHEAD

While an entity knows with virtual certainty the amount and cost of direct materials and direct labor that goes into making a product, such is not the case with factory overhead.[17] Numerous factors compose factory overheard (e.g., indirect raw materials, indirect labor, depreciation on buildings and equipment, taxes on factory property, and so forth). Moreover, both fixed and variable cost components compose factory overhead. Further complicating matters is that the firm may not know some of the overhead cost aspects when production commences, or during the production cycle. The accounting system compensates for these factors by applying factory overhead on a predetermined basis. One computes an **applied factory overhead rate** in the following manner:

Applied factory overhead rate = estimated total factory overhead costs / activity base

The **activity base** is a logical factor that causes overhead to occur. Accountants term such a factor as the **cost driver** because that specific activity *drives* overhead costs. Direct labor hours or machine hours are examples of cost drivers. A labor-intensive specialty woodworking operation, for example, would probably use direct labor hours as its activity base. The entity's factory overhead costs would be related to (or correlated with) the numbers of hours the craftspeople work in such an environment. A highly automated manufacturer, on the other hand, could use machine hours as its basis for applying factory overhead. Machine hours in this case would *drive* or cause overhead costs to exist.

Readers should bear in mind that firms compute applied factory overhead rates *before* they begin production. The activity base, like the factory overhead costs, is a forecast of anticipated activity during the production period (i.e., the expected number of labor or machine hours that the firm thinks it will work). Once the entity computes its activity base, the firm applies factory overhead costs to direct material and direct labor to determine the overall cost of a job. It does so by multiplying the applied factory overhead rate by the amount of activity used during the process.

STANDARD COSTING

A firm estimates the cost of a specific job by projecting total direct material, direct labor, and applied factory overhead costs. Accountants calculate a **standard product cost** by dividing expected units of production into the forecast of the total job cost. Thus, a standard cost is determined for one unit of output.

The following example demonstrates how a firm implements standard product cost accounting under a job order cost system. Assume that the production standards for the only product of Redlands Embroidery Services, Inc. (RES) are as follows:

Product	Expected Production and Sales	Direct Materials Cost per Unit	Direct Labor Cost per Hour	Direct Labor per Unit of Production
Clothing	5,000 units	$4	$10	2 hours

RES expects 2010 factory overhead costs to total $30,000.[18] The firm applies factory overhead based on direct labor hours because of the labor-intensive process of sewing script onto articles of clothing. Therefore, the *applied* overhead rate is $3 per direct labor hour ($30,000 / 10,000 total direct labor hours). Another way to consider applied factory overhead is that RES applies it at the rate of $6 per embroidered item ($30,000 of factory overhead costs divided by 5,000 clothing units).

Exhibit 5-5A presents the company's standard product costs as follows:

Exhibit 5-5A
Redlands Embroidery Service
Standard Product Costs

Item	Clothing Item
Direct materials—$4 per unit	$ 4

Direct labor—2 DLH * $10 per hour	20
Factory overhead—2 DLH @ $3 per hour	6
Product cost	**$30**

A JOB-ORDER-COSTING EXAMPLE

The accounting system enables an entity to measure and communicate financial information in the manner outlined in Chapter 1. The next two exhibits present the beginning point (journal entries) and ending point (financial statement effects) of the accounting cycle for the standard job order costing system.

Exhibit 5-5B
Redlands Embroidery Service
Job Order Costing Journal Entries

Trans.	Accounts	Debit	Credit
1.	Work in process inventory ($4 * 5,000)	20,000	
	Raw materials inventory		20,000
2.	Work in process inventory ($20 * 5,000)	100,000	
	Cash		100,000
3.	Work in process inventory ($6 * 5,000)	30,000	
	Overhead applied		30,000
4.	Actual overhead (determined at the end of production)	30,000	
	Cash		30,000

One interprets each journal entry for Exhibit 5-5B as follows:
1. Transfer raw materials inventory (thread and related items) into production.
2. Add direct labor costs to work in process inventory and pay for those costs.
3. Apply factory overhead to work in process inventory.
4. Pay for the actual factory overhead (assuming actual overhead costs equal budgeted overhead).

Let us assume that RES sells 3,500 embroidered items for $40 each. Exhibit 5-5C presents the job order cost accounting system's effects on the financial statements:

Exhibit 5-5C
Redlands Embroidery Service
2010 Financial Statement Excerpts

Income Statement:	
Revenues ($40 * 3,500)	$140,000
Cost of goods sold ($30 * 3,500)	<u>105,000</u>
Gross profit	$35,000
Balance Sheet:	
Current Assets:	
Inventory ($30 * 1,500)	$45,000

Firms do not always meet their budgeted expectations. The actual cost of materials, labor, and overhead may deviate from their predetermined standards. These departures are especially true for factory overhead. For example, RES may actually incur more or less than $30,000 of factory overhead during the production period. A number of reasons could account for the variance. For instance, the firm could:

- produce more than or less than the expected 5,000 units of clothing.
- spend a different amount of time for direct labor on each article of clothing than the forecast 2 direct labor hours per unit.
- experience unforeseen changes in the cost of specific factory overhead items.

FACTORY OVERHEAD

Two related issues exist when an entity applies overhead costs to jobs. First, unlike the preceding exhibits (5-5A through 5-5C), an entity undertakes numerous jobs during an accounting period. Second, as we note after Exhibit 5-5C, the actual amount of factory overhead incurred a reporting period will probably not equal the amount of factory overhead applied to those jobs. We illustrate the accounting for these two related circumstances in the following example.

Assume for the moment that Redlands, Inc. begins three jobs in the current reporting period. No beginning or ending inventory related to these jobs exists. Exhibit 5-6A presents the data related to the jobs:

Exhibit 5-6A
Job Cost Data

	Job #1	Job #2	Job #3	Total
Direct materials	$1	$3	$2	$6
Direct labor	6	2	4	12
Applied factory overhead	3	1	2	6
Product cost (per unit)	$10	$6	$8	$24
Quantity produced	5	10	5	20
Job cost	$50	$60	$40	$150

Redlands completes all three jobs during the current accounting period. It sells Jobs #1 and #2, but Job #3 remains in finished goods inventory. Redlands sold its products at a 50% markup over cost. Actual factory overhead costs for the period totaled $50.

Exhibit 5-6B presents the journal entries related to each job and the summary journal entries beginning with the transfer of inventory to finished goods:

Exhibit 5-6B
Journal Entries

Trans.	Accounts	Job #1	Job #2	Job #3	Total
1	Finished goods inventory	50	60	40	150
	Work in process inventory	50	60	40	150
2	Accounts receivable	75	90	N/A	165
	Sales revenues	75	90	N/A	165
3	Cost of goods sold	50	60	N/A	110
	Finished goods inventory	50	60	N/A	110
4	Factory overhead—actual	N/A	N/A	N/A	50
	Materials, cash, accumulated depr., etc.	N/A	N/A	N/A	50

5	Cost of goods sold	N/A	N/A	N/A	11
	Factory overhead	N/A	N/A	N/A	11
6	Finished goods inventory	N/A	N/A	N/A	4
	Factory overhead	N/A	N/A	N/A	4

Transaction 1 transfers the inventory to finished goods from work in process. Transactions 2 and 3 record the sale of Jobs #1 and #2 and match their costs (on an applied factory overhead basis) against recognized revenues. Transaction 4 records the actual amount of factory overhead. Note that the offsetting credit in this entry is to multiple accounts (i.e., materials for indirect material costs, cash paid for indirect labor, and accumulated depreciation for the depreciation on the manufacturing facility and its equipment).

Note that total *actual* overhead is $50 and total *applied* overhead (to all three jobs) is $35. In this instance, Redlands did not apply enough factory overhead to its three jobs ($50 vs. $35). The firm must account for actual overhead as part of its products' costs. It does so by apportioning the under application of factory overhead to cost of goods sold and finished goods inventory. Therefore, the firm adds $11 to cost of goods sold (transaction 5), because the sold jobs (numbers 1 and 2) comprised 11/15 of the total applied production costs ($110 out of $150). Transaction 6 adjusts finished goods inventory by $4 for the remaining factory overhead variance because it relates to the unsold Job #3, which comprises the remaining 4/15 of the total applied production costs ($40/$150).

Exhibit 5-6C presents the relevant financial statements disclosures:

Exhibit 5-6C
Financial Statements

Income Statement	
Revenues	$165
Cost of goods sold ($110 + 11)	<u>121</u>
Gross profit	$44
Balance Sheet	
Current assets:	
Finished goods inventory ($40 + 4)	$44

ACTIVITY-BASED COSTING

The preceding discussion related to job order costing systems (Exhibits 5-5A–5-6C) is overly simplistic, because it allocated all factory overhead costs based on direct labor hours. Implicitly, this allocation method assumed that direct labor hours caused (or drove) all factory overhead costs to exist. In reality, many activities drive factory overhead costs, even for the simplest product. Sound cost accounting systems, therefore, consider all of those key elements that drive or cause product costs to occur and incorporate them into the product costing system. Failure to do so misprices the actual product cost. Such a failure can lead to significant incorrect managerial decisions. A firm that severely underestimates the true cost of a product, due to an under application of factory overhead, may end up selling that product at a price that is less than it cost to produce. Conversely, a company that applies too much factory overhead to a product's cost could lose sales because the artificially high product cost would result in overpriced products that people would not purchase.

Activity-based costing (ABC) is a systematic approach that seeks to identify and apply all of the diverse factors that affect the cost of a product. ABC accounts for the multiple cost drivers that consume entity resources, rather than relying on a single cost driver. By identifying all significant cost drivers, or activities, an ABC system validly relates consumed resources to production costs.

IMPLEMENTING ACTIVITY-BASED COSTING

Perhaps the greatest advantage of activity-based costing is that firms can apply an ABC system to any cost object. Accountants define a **cost object** as anything for which management desires financial cost data. In the preceding Redlands Embroidery Service example, the cost object was an embroidered clothing item. A cost object, however, is not necessarily a physical good—it could also be the cost of providing a service to a customer.

Reduced to its essence, activity-based costing is a four-step process that helps measure the cost of specific cost objects. These steps are as follows:

1. Identify and define critical activities that drive costs.
2. Gather relevant cost data for the drivers.
3. Assign costs (overhead or otherwise) to cost pools.
4. Assign costs to specific cost objects.

For ease of understanding, we will now apply activity-based costing to service-related cost objects rather than to manufactured products.[19]

ABC EXAMPLE

The executive management team for the Bank of Redlands (or the "Bank") in conjunction with its internal accounting staff seeks to implement activity-based accounting for customer services at its branch offices. The Bank wants to determine how much it costs to provide key services to its customers so that it can assess its competitive position in the marketplace.

Step 1. Identify and define critical activities that drive costs

After carefully studying operations at each branch office, the Bank concludes that four activities drive labor costs in a branch office.

1. opening accounts
2. processing routine customer deposits and withdrawals
3. handling non-routine customer transactions
4. making managerial decisions

Step 2. Gather relevant cost data for the drivers

The branch office classifies three types of labor costs (job descriptions):

1. Tellers
2. Customer Representatives
3. Manager

The Bank gathers the following labor salaries (costs) for its university branch office:

Tellers	$150,000
Customer Representatives	70,000
Manager	85,000
Total	$305,000

After careful observation of employee work habits, interviews with the workers about their job demands, and time-and-motion studies, the Bank distributes work effort across activities in the following percentages:

Job Function	Open Accounts	Routine Transactions	Non-Routine Transactions	Managerial Decisions	Total
Tellers	10%	75%	15%	0%	100%
Reps.	50%	15%	30%	5%	100%
Manager	0%	0%	20%	80%	100%

Step 3. Assign costs to cost pools

The Bank constructs a table containing activities and job descriptions. It multiplies a job's cost (e.g., tellers salaries) by the percentage of time that job devotes to an activity (e.g., routine deposit and withdrawal transactions) in order to determine the amounts in the table. One then determines a cost pool by summing the cell amounts in a specific column. The following table presents the amounts in each of the four activity's cost pools:

Job	Open Accounts	Routine Deposits / Withdrawals	Non-Routine Transactions	Managerial Decisions	Totals
Tellers	150 *.10 = $15,000	150*.75= $112,500	150*.15= $22,500	150*.0= $0	$150,000
Reps	70*.50= $35,000	70*.15= $10,500	70*.30= $21,000	70*.5= $3,500	70,000
Manager	85*0= $0	85*.0= $0	85*.20= $17,000	85*.80= $68,000	85,000
Cost Pool	$50,000	$123,000	$60,500	$71,500	$305,000

The reader of the table should note that both the bottom row (cost pools) and rightmost column (totals for job descriptions) equal $305,000.

Step 4. Assign costs to cost objects

Internal branch records provide the amount of activity for each cost pool. This allows the bank to determine an **activity rate**, which equals the cost of the cost object. In our case, we have four cost objects—opening accounts, routine transactions, non-routine transactions, and managerial decisions.[20] In order to implement step four, one divides the amount in a specific cost pool by its total activity to determine the cost per activity.

In the table below, for example, the university branch of the Bank of Redlands opened 1,750 new accounts during the reporting period. The total cost of providing that customer service was $50,000, according to the cost pool calculation. The cost for opening an account, on average, was $28.57 ($50,000 / 1,750).

Cost Object	$ in Cost Pool	Total Activities	Activity Rate
Open Accounts	$50,000	1,750 new accounts	$28.57
Routine Transactions	$123,000	198,000 transactions	$ .621
Non-Routine Transactions	$60,500	1,322 transactions	$45.76
Managerial Decisions	$71,500	905 decisions	$79.00

ACTIVITY-BASED COSTING IMPLICATIONS

Managers use activity-based costing to price products, assess market competitiveness, and develop greater efficiencies. In short, ABC helps the firm by providing managers with relevant data inputs for making decisions. Entities can trend performance over time and against competition to measure their effectiveness and make the necessary adjustments. Assume for the moment that the Bank of Redlands compiled activity rates for all of its branches and accessed reliable industry standards from a banking association. Exhibit 5-7 presents the cost data for the university branch, the Bank as a whole, and the industry norms.

Exhibit 5-7
Bank of Redlands
Activity-Based Cost Data

Activity (Cost Object)	University Branch Rates	Bank of Redlands Mean Rates	Industry Mean Rates
Open Accounts	$28.57	$27.88	$27.25
Routine Transactions	.621	.585	.552
Non-Routine Transactions	45.76	42.68	39.51
Managerial Decisions	79.00	75.30	69.57

One would infer from the data in Exhibit 5-7 that the Bank of Redlands is less efficient than its competition, and that its university branch office lags overall Bank of Redlands performance standards. By identifying and benchmarking the relevant cost activities, activity-based costing provides management with valid cost data—the first step in formulating a corrective action plan.

Summary

Chapter 5 examined the various aspects of the concept of cost. It classified, defined, and implemented critical cost dimensions in order to improve managerial decisions. Two elements composed this chapter: cost factors and cost systems. We began our discussion of cost factors by differentiating between revenue and capital expenditures. Next, we contrasted product costs to period costs with an emphasis on how each cost category affects a manufacturer's financial statements. Knowledge of product costs, coupled with an understanding of fixed and variable cost behavior, enables the manager to appreciate how variable-cost income statements align managerial performance with overall corporate goals. The extents to which managers can control cost, contain cost across product mix, and appreciate opportunity cost, also improve managerial decisions.

The second section of this chapter focused on product costing. It addressed the need for applying factory overhead to costs and computing the application rate. Managers incorporate applied factory overhead to direct material and direct labor costs when establishing standard product costs. Once an entity establishes its production standards, the accounting system gathers and communicates cost and sales information as products wend through the manufacturing process. Chapter 5 illustrates such accounting procedures with examples from job-order costing and activity-based costing.

Key Terms

Absorption costing
Activity base
Activity rate
Activity-based costing (ABC)
Applied factory overhead rate
Capital (asset) expenditure
Controllable costs
Conversion costs
Cost
Cost driver
Cost object
Cost of goods manufactured
Discretionary costs
Expense
Fixed cost
Full-cost (absorption-cost) income statement
Gross profit margin
Job-order costing
Opportunity cost
Period costs
Prime costs
Process costing
Product costs
Product mix
Revenue expenditure
Standard product cost
Sunk cost
Uncontrollable costs
Variable cost
Variable costing
Variable-cost income statement

Assignments

Accounting Concepts Crossword

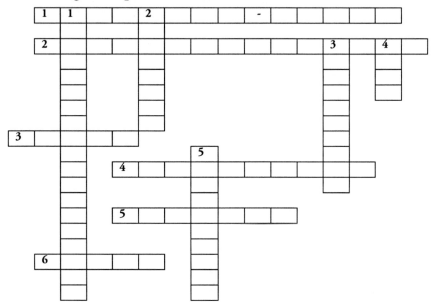

Across

[1] A systematic costing approach that seeks to identify and apply all of the diverse factors that affect the cost of a product.

[2] What is it called when an entity invests in a particular asset, and therefore foregoes the opportunity to use those funds to acquire another resource.

[3] A cost that remains constant in total dollar amount, regardless of activity level.

[4] GAAP requires allocating all product costs, both fixed and variable, to the income statement for the portion of inventory sold in the reporting period, and to the balance sheet for the unsold amount. Accountants commonly refer to this treatment as _____ costing.

[5] Inventory-related expenditures.

[6] The expenditures directly identified with the production of finished goods (direct materials and direct labor) are _____ costs.

Down

[1] Economic sacrifices that produce future periods' revenues as well as present ones; therefore, an entity allocates such costs as expenses over multiple reporting periods.

[2] A _____ cost remains constant in monetary amount on a per unit basis, regardless of activity.

[3] Direct labor and factory overhead are called _____ costs.

[4] Transacted costs are _____ costs.

[5] The logical factor that causes overhead to occur.

DISCUSSION ITEMS

What Would Your Accountant Say?

Your company has incurred several million dollars of research and development (R&D) costs during the year, and according to GAAP these costs must be expensed as incurred. This expense will cause the company to show a loss on its current period income statement. The CEO does not understand the accounting principles dealing with "revenue" vs. "capital" expenditures in general, and specifically would like to know why these R&D costs could not be put on the balance sheet, since he feels they have value that extends beyond the current year. What would your accountant say to the CEO?

Theory vs. Practice

The theory of activity-based-costing (ABC) was developed in the manufacturing sector of the United States in the 1980s. Although originally designed for use in manufacturing, in practice, ABC has proven to be a useful tool for allocating costs in other industries as well, as demonstrated in this chapter. Use your own background and work experience to describe some situations where ABC might provide a valuable alternative to more traditional cost allocation methodologies.

PROBLEMS

Problem 5-1

The cost accounting system for Ontario Manufacturing, Inc. gathers the following cost data for 2010 (dollar amounts in thousands).

Raw materials inventory:
(All raw materials are direct materials)

Beginning inventory	$14
Purchases of raw materials	121
Ending inventory	9

Work in process inventory:

Beginning work in process	25
Ending work in process	38

Finished goods inventory:

Beginning finished goods	66
Ending finished goods	36

Other data:

Direct labor costs	155
Factory overhead costs	62
Sales revenues	600
Selling, general, and administrative expenses	184
Accounts receivable	72
Accounts payable	41
Income tax rate	30%
Number of shares of stock (in thousands)	20

Required:

    a.   Construct Ontario's cost of goods manufactured statement.

    b.   Present the firm's income statement in proper form.

    c.   Disclose inventory on the December 31, 2010 balance sheet.

Problem 5-2

Riverside, Inc. accumulated the following data for the sole product produced by Department A for 2010, its first year of business:

Sales	260 units @ $30
Variable product costs	$12 per unit
Fixed product costs	$2,880
Units manufactured	360 units

Required:

    a.   Compute Riverside's 2010 full-cost (absorption) and variable-cost income statements through gross profit.

    b.   Report Riverside's 2010 ending inventory under both costing approaches.

    c.   Assume that Riverside agrees to pay a 10% bonus to the manager of Department A based on the amount of gross profit that is in the best interest of the firm. Compute the amount of the bonus.

Problem 5-3

The Temecula Bauble and Trinket Company make two products that reflect its corporate name. The firm is capital-intensive and applies factory overhead based on machine hours. The cost accountant gathers the following data related to its products:

Item	Bauble	Trinket
Budgeted production	2,000 baubles	6,000 trinkets
Direct materials per unit	$2.00	$1.00
Direct labor cost per unit	$.50	$.25
Machine hours per unit	2 hours	3 hours

In addition, Temecula anticipates $17,600 of total factory overhead costs during the period. Temecula learns at the end of the accounting period that actual factory overhead costs totaled $19,000.

Required:

a.   Compute the applied factory overhead rate.

b.   Determine the standard cost per bauble and trinket.

c.   Assume that actual production levels and costs equal budgeted expectations for direct materials and labor. Record the job order costing journal entries for both products.

d.   Compute cost of goods sold and ending inventory (on an applied factory overhead basis) if Temecula sells 75% of its baubles and 60% of its trinkets. (Assume the firm has no beginning inventory.)

e.   Account for the difference between applied and actual factory overhead costs by adjusting cost of goods sold and finished goods inventory.

Case 5-1

GLO, Inc. recently hired you as its chief financial officer and charged you with developing a sound economic basis for billing its services. The issue centers on determining the cost for each of the three job types that the company provides to its customers.

Background

The company began operations in 1985 as a painting contractor. Its two founding partners, a husband and wife team, quickly realized that a more lucrative market existed for removing toxic lead-based painted surfaces from homes and commercial buildings. Numerous governmental entities were enacting legislation that required property owners to remove all traces of lead paint when refurbishing their buildings. The market demanded lead paint removal!

Lead paint removal is a complex, potentially hazardous, time consuming, and expensive task; consequently, it is best left to specialists in the field. It was against this backdrop that Jack and Susan Serna formed GLO, Inc., which stands for Get the Lead Out. Jack Serna developed technical proficiencies in removing lead paint through educational courses, an apprenticeship with an out-of-state company, and trial and error. Susan relied on her marketing background to secure lead paint removal contracts. She also serves as the operational officer for the business.

The company rapidly developed an outstanding reputation and grew quickly. The proliferation of jobs resulted in exponentially increasing revenues in the last decade and required significant hiring and training of personal. While somewhat profitable, the owners felt as though income and cash flows were not commensurate with revenues. Jack stated, "We're busier and busier all the time and we continually work harder than ever, but our bottom line doesn't reflect it."

Susan expressed concern that job costing and product pricing contributed to the lack of profitability. "It seems to me that we are out of balance," she said. "We know that certain jobs are more intense than other ones are, but we bid them out equally. That just doesn't seem to make sense."

Her husband continued. "You're right. In the old days, we just replaced plaster walls and ceilings with new drywall for homeowners. Those jobs are *routine*. Now, a lot of our business is corporate. These folks have very specific concerns, because they have to answer to more regulatory agencies than home owners do. In addition, companies often occupy older buildings where we have to manually remove lead-based paint from the wood trim and apply non-lead paint to those surfaces, rather than just gutting the walls. These jobs are definitely *non-routine*."

Susan added, "Not only that, but I've been securing contracts to redo historic homes. The lead removal work on those properties is even more time-consuming than that required for our corporate clients. The detail work required for historic homes is unbelievable. It eats time like crazy. I'd say these restorations are *extraordinary* jobs."

The Serna's subsequently met with Roger Howland, their job estimator, and Jose Lima, who supervises the paint removal crews. Roger liked the current system and wanted to maintain it. He contended the GLO should continue bidding out jobs at $29.13 per square foot. "Look, we've been through the accounting data a dozen times. The average cost of lead paint removal is $24.28 per square foot. Our twenty percent markup over costs gives us enough wiggle room if a few jobs take extra time."

Jose countered, "Easy for you to say, Rog, you don't have to deal with these difficult jobs. You just do a one-time walkthrough and measure the square footage. My crews have to do the work. It takes time for them to handle a challenging job, but they know they don't have it because we bill by the foot. This creates a strong incentive to rush jobs that require a lot of time. The result is often less than perfect."

Howland remained steadfast. "It isn't a perfect world, Jose. I say if it ain't broke, don't fix it."

Data

After listening to the discussion, the reader tends to believe that the way GLO costs its services and bids for contracts is, indeed, broken and needs fixing. Begin by gathering cost information from the firm's accounting system, and summarize these expenses in the following table:

Exhibit 1

Expense Account	Amount
Wages, salaries, and benefits	$4,975,000
Site-related supplies	880,000
Disposal fees	2,423,000
Insurance	648,000
Business licenses	96,000
Equipment depreciation	418,000
Miscellaneous expenses	270,000
Total expenses	$9,710,000

Then identify the critical jobs or activities in the company's operations. Next, determine the item that drives each one of those activities. These efforts lead the reader to construct the next exhibit:

Exhibit 2

Job (Activity)	Activity Measure	Total Activity
Estimation	Number of total jobs	320
Size	Square feet	400,000
Setup	Number of total jobs	320
Non-routine (trim stripping)	Number of non-routine jobs	96
Extraordinary (historical detailing)	Number of extraordinary jobs	41
Other	Number of total jobs	320

After identifying the activities and their cost drivers, conduct a series of in-depth interviews with personnel to find out how much time and effort they spend on various tasks. Complement those interviews by observing how people work on various jobs and relate those tasks to corporate expenses. Compile a table distributing resources consumed across activities based on interviews and studies.

Exhibit 3 presents the distribution table:

Exhibit 3

	Estimation	Size	Setup	Non-routine	Extra-ordinary	Other	Total
Wages	5%	20%	5%	30%	35%	5%	100%
Supplies	0%	40%	15%	20%	15%	10%	100%
Disposal fees	5%	25%	5%	30%	30%	5%	100%
Insurance	5%	20%	5%	20%	45%	5%	100%
Licenses	5%	60%	20%	5%	5%	5%	100%
Depreciation	5%	55%	5%	20%	10%	5%	100%
Miscellaneous	5%	70%	5%	10%	5%	5%	100%

Each project requires one site visit (estimate), one precise measurement (job size), and one job setup, regardless of whether the job is *routine, non-routine,* or *extraordinary.* In addition, each job absorbs a portion of the costs associated with the miscellaneous (other) activities.

Required:

The goal is to prepare a memorandum to Susan and Jack Serna that covers the following points:
1. Why the current job costing formula is unacceptable.
2. Why the firm needs to institute activity-based costing (ABC).
3. The cost of a 1,000 square foot *routine*, *non-routine*, and *extraordinary* job, based on both GLO's current costing practice, and the proposed ABC approach.
4. The contract bid price for each one of those job types based on both GLO's current costing practice, and the proposed ABC approach.

The memo will be in the form of an executive summary not to exceed two double-spaced pages. Present all calculations, tables, and so forth, supporting the above four points as attachments to the memo. Make parenthetical references to them as needed in the executive summary. The attachments should at least include the allocation of costs to activity cost pools, and the activity rates for the activity cost pools.

Endnotes

1. "Elements of Financial Statements," *Statement of Financial Accounting Concepts* No. 6, paragraph 26, note 19. (Stamford, CT: FASB, 1985)

2. This statement assumes a for-profit firm.

3. It is axiomatic in accounting that the expenses follow revenues.

4. As noted earlier in the chapter, managerial judgment affects capital expenditure disclosures. For instance, Extreme Edge's management selects the depreciation method and estimates the economic life of its equipment.

5. "Accounting for Research and Development Costs," *Statement of Financial Accounting Standards* No. 2. (Stamford, CT: FASB, 1974)

6. The uncertainties extend beyond the probability of the success R&D efforts. For instance, the amount and timing of future revenues and cash flows generated from successful R&D efforts are difficult, if not impossible, to measure.

7. This statement is true so long as R&D increases over time. If such costs were consistent from year to year, then amortization of R&D expenditures would eventually approximate their immediate write-off.

8. A firm offering services does not report inventory for resale; consequently, it does not have cost of goods sold.

9. Companies often differentiate inventory categories in a footnote, rather than on the face of the balance sheet.

10. This discussion assumes, for the sake of simplicity, that all raw materials used in the manufacturing process are *direct* materials. In reality, some raw materials consumed are *indirect* materials. Indirect materials are part of factory overhead and not a direct material cost.

11. Economic theory dictates that all costs are variable in the long run. Many costs, however, remain fixed within a relevant range of activity. We assume that managerial decisions will occur within a relevant fixed-cost range.

12. This discussion simplifies cost behavior by ignoring such complexities as curvilinear relationships.

13. We revisit cost behavior for decision-making purposes in detail in Chapter 6.

14. Variable cost income statements technically do not use the term gross profit. They refer to the difference between revenues and variable expenses as contribution margin. Chapter 6 will discuss variable cost income statements and contribution margins in detail.

15. Cost control, to a certain extent, is a continuum. For example, Extreme Edge has some degree of control over the timing and payment of inventory. Moreover, it can affect inventory costs by negotiating with vendors or seeking goods from other suppliers.

16. Chapter 4 introduced the concept of opportunity cost within the context of equity cost of capital.

17. Deviations do occur from the budget. We address such variances in Chapter 7.

18. This treatment of overhead grossly simplifies many of the cost accounting issues regarding overhead. For example, the charge to *actual* factory overhead pertains to many production jobs, not just a single job. Moreover, we do not distinguish between fixed and variable overhead costs at this time. The intent of this example is to demonstrate that the firm must apply overhead to each job as it takes place. Chapter 7 will address variances between applied and actual factory overhead.

19. The application of ABC to the manufacturing environment is procedurally very complex.

20. In this simple example, the cost drivers equal the cost objects. Such is not the case in more complex applications of activity-based costing.

Chapter 6

Budgeting

CHAPTER LEARNING OBJECTIVES

Upon completion of this chapter, readers should be able to:

> Articulate the need for operating and capital budgets within an enterprise.

> Compile a comprehensive master budget.

> Derive pro forma financial statements from the numerous elements of the master budget.

> Analyze cost-volume-profit data in order to understand cost behavior and target profit levels.

> Assess the effect of income taxes on profit projections and net profit margin forecasts.

> Account for individual product, and overall product mix, costs and profits when an entity sells multiple products.

Management decision making is primarily a forward-looking endeavor. While organizational executives can learn from past decisions, they cannot change them. They are, in the parlance of the previous chapter, sunk costs. Wealth creation requires managers to deploy existing assets effectively and acquire future ones selectively. Managers must carefully plan their investment strategies and control them in order to achieve optimal results. Budgets are critical to successful resource allocation. A budget financially expresses management's expectations about some aspect of corporate performance, economic position, or cash flow. The accounting system provides the necessary financial inputs for budgetary compilation and allows management to monitor actual results against budgeted expectations.

This chapter explores the role of the accounting system in the budgeting process. It focuses on budget compilation and profit planning; the next and final chapter of this text evaluates actual performance relative to budgeted expectations. We begin this chapter by evaluating the components of an integrated budget and demonstrating critical aspects of budget compilation. This process culminates in an articulated set of budgeted financial statements. The second half of this chapter focuses on profit planning. It examines how managers quantify their expectations for creating wealth. An entity budgets, after all, as part of its pursuit of profit.[1] Targeting income levels, therefore, enumerates goals that managers factor into their budgets.

BUDGETS

A **budget** quantifies managerial expectations about the future. The timeline of the budget can vary from a daily budget to one that extends many years into the future. We simplify this continuum by dichotomizing budgets into operating and capital budgets.

An **operating budget** pertains to one fiscal reporting period, be it a month, quarter, or year. Befitting its name, operating budgets focus on quantifying the near term expectations of the firm's core or central business activities. One element of an operating budget, for example, is the quantification of the amount and timing of cash collected from credit sales. Conversely, a **capital budget** extends beyond one year and revolves around the financing and investing activities necessary for sustainable business operations. Constructing a manufacturing facility and floating debt to finance such a project illustrate elements of capital budgeting. We focus our attention on operating budgets in this text, due to the inherent complexities in capital budgeting.[2]

BUDGETING CONSIDERATIONS

Budgets affect everyone and everything within an organization. Consequently, managers must be aware of their affect on people and other resources. A good manager adheres to sound budgeting principles in order to the meet the organization's mission effectively, efficiently, and productively. The following list presents some of the more prevalent aspects of good budgeting:

- *Realism.* Budgets should realistically quantify future operating performance. Unrealistically optimistic budgets can create dysfunctional behavior, and overly pessimistic ones reduce incentives to achieve at a high level.
- *Environment.* Good budgets include external factors. Sound budgets require the firm to consider such elements as the state of the economy and the health of the industry, as well as the internal productive capabilities of the organization.

- *Range.* Forecasting the future is inherently imprecise; consequently, the entity should establish a feasible range of budgeted expectations. One simple method is to prepare a best, worst, and most likely operating budget.
- *Participation.* All those affected by a budget should have input into the budgeting process. Obviously, management sets the budget, but employee participation helps managers create realistic budgets and increases employee *buy in* of the budgeting process and the budgets themselves.
- *Appropriateness.* Detail and specificity of a budget should match managerial need. For example, the plant manager of a large multinational requires detailed production budgets, but the CEO only needs summarized data pertaining to each factory's productivity.
- *Integration.* Each portion of the operating budget should use data from those portions of the budget that precede it. A specific portion of the operating budget also serves as an input for those budgetary segments that follow it in the budgeting sequence.
- *Continuation.* Budgeting is continual process, which the organization should roll forward from period to period. For example, assume policy requires budgeting for the four quarters of 2010 by the end of 2009. Upon completion of the first fiscal quarter of 2010, the entity should prepare a budget for the first quarter of 2011.
- *Feedback.* Management must always compare budgeted expectations with actual results. They should identify variances and correct budgetary deviations, whenever economically feasible to do so.[3]

BUDGETING PROCESS

The **master budget** is a comprehensive operating budget that begins with a sales forecast and concludes with pro forma financial statements. These budgeted financial statements reflect the operating performance, financial position, and cash flows of the entity as if the budget unfolds as predicted. The critical steps in constructing a comprehensive operating budgeting for a *manufacturing* firm are as follows:[4]

1. Sales budget
2. Production budget
3. Purchases budget
4. Cash budget
5. Pro forma financial statements

The general approach used when constructing all budgets within the operating budget process is to determine physical quantity initially. Once the firm determines quantity, it multiplies those physical amounts by the appropriate monetary values.

SALES BUDGETS

Sales budgets are the vital first step in the process, because all other budgets within the master operating budget stem from the sales forecast. The firm must first know the quantity of products it anticipates selling during the budgeted period in order to determine the other aspects of a master budget. Marketing and sales departments provide significant input into the sales budget. The accounting function uses this information to compile forecast quantity. It then attaches specific unit prices to complete the sales budget.

One can dichotomize sales forecasting techniques into those based on mathematical (statistical) models, and those derived from informed judgment. Some of the more prevalent statistical models include the following:

- **Trend analysis**. One forecasts sales by extrapolating from the amount and direction of historical revenue levels. One example of trending sales is **linear regression analysis**. The forecaster statistically fits a trend line that minimizes the distance between historical sales levels and the reporting periods in which they occurred. Regressing sales over time enables one to forecast sales levels mathematically.
- **Exponential smoothing**. This method is similar to trend analysis; however, the forecaster places greater statistical weight on more recent sales levels than those from distant accounting periods.
- **Decomposition**. One forecasts sales by including statistical measures for **cyclicality** (sensitivity to changes in the overall economy), **seasonality** (changes in activity levels within one reporting period), and **randomness** (unpredictable events), in addition to trend analysis.

Informed opinion of future events is the basis for **judgmental sales forecasting**. This approach combines professional judgment with relevant and reliable economic, industry, competitor, and corporate information in order to forecast sales. A manager should use judgment unless he or she is thoroughly familiar with quantitative forecasting methods. Both statistical and judgmental approaches can provide vital insights about future sales levels. Consequently, a manager who is well versed in statistically forecasting should quantitatively forecast sales and temper those forecasts with professional judgment.

BUDGETING ILLUSTRATED

The following integrated example demonstrates compilation of a master budget. Assume that Redlands Manufacturing, Inc. (RMI) budgets operations for its sole product in July 2010. Exhibit 6-1A presents the data related to the sales forecast, product cost, and June 30 balance sheet:

Exhibit 6-1A
Redlands Manufacturing, Inc.
Budgetary Data

Unit sales forecast	35,000
Sales price per unit	$ 20.00
Forecast sales revenues	$700,000
Standard Product Cost:	
Direct materials (3 ounces @ $2.00 per ounce)	$ 6.00
Direct labor	4.00
Factory overhead	2.00
Standard product cost per unit	$12.00

Balance Sheet

June 30, 2010

Assets			Liabilities	
Cash	$150,000		Current liabilities	$0
Accounts receivable	100,000		Long-term liabilities	
Raw materials inventory	108,000		Bonds payable	$270,000
Finished goods inventory	120,000			
Total current assets	478,000		Shareholders' Equity	
			Common stock	300,000
Equipment, net of depreciation	372,000		Retained earnings	280,000
Total assets	$850,000		Total liabilities and s/ equity	$850,000

Expected sales drive production budgets within manufacturing firms. Productive capabilities usually exceed sales forecasts in the near term. Consequently, the production budget centers on insuring that adequate finished goods inventory exists to meet anticipated sales demand. In the event that sales demand exceeds capacity, management must determine whether to acquire additional resources or alter sales budgets.

We now demonstrate the compilation of a production budget.[5] Recall from Chapter 5 the cost of goods sold section as it relates to a manufacturer's income statement:

Income Statement:	**Cost of Goods Sold Section:**
Sales revenues	Beginning inventory of finished goods
-Cost of goods sold	+Cost of goods manufactured
Gross margin	= Goods available for sale
-S,G, and A expenses	-Ending inventory of finished goods
Pretax income	= Cost of goods sold

The accountant uses the cost of goods sold section to construct a **production budget**. RMI had 10,000 units on hand at the end of June. We know this because the firm reports $120,000 of finished goods inventory on its June 30, 2010 balance sheet, and the standard product cost is $12.00 per unit ($120,000 / $12.00 = 10,000 units of finished goods). Management decides that the firm must maintain an ending monthly inventory of 3,000 units plus 20% of the sales forecast for the next month. (The firm forecasts 40,000 units of sales in August.) Exhibit 6-1B presents the July 2010 production budget.

Exhibit 6-1B
Production Budget (in units)

	July
Beginning inventory of finished goods (given)	10,000
+ Goods manufactured	Z
Goods available for sale	Y
- Ending inventory of finished goods	X
Goods sold (per the sales forecast)	35,000

One solves for X, Y, and Z in order.

The computations for July are as follows:

$$X = 3,000 + .20(40,000) = 11,000 \text{ (per management directive)}$$
$$Y = 35,000 + 11,000 = 46,000$$
$$Z = 46,000 - 10,000 = 36,000$$

RMI must produce 36,000 units during July in order to meet forecast demand and required inventory levels. One would continue the approach in succeeding months—remembering that the ending inventory of one month becomes the beginning inventory for the next one. Exhibit 6-1C presents the forecast of the July 2010 cost of production:

Exhibit 6-1C
Production Budget (in dollars)

	July
Goods manufactured	36,000
* Standard cost per unit	$ 12.00
Cost of goods manufactured	$432,000

Recall from Exhibit 6-1A that it takes three (3) units of raw material inputs (ounces) to produce one (1) unit of output. Assume company policy requires the ending raw materials inventory to equal 50% of next month's production needs, and further assume that the company budgets 42,000 units of production for August. You budget for the purchase of raw materials as follows:

Exhibit 6-1D
Purchases Budget (in units)

	July
Beginning raw materials inventory (per the balance sheet)	54,000
+Raw materials purchased	Z
= Total raw materials needed	Y
-Ending raw materials inventory	X
= Raw materials needed for production	108,000

RMI has 54,000 units of raw materials at the beginning of July because its June balance sheet discloses $108,000 of raw materials inventory and each ounce of raw material costs $2.00. Similarly, the firm needs 108,000 units of raw materials for production, because the production budget in Exhibit 6-1B budgets 36,000 units of output and the firm requires three (3) ounces of input to produce one unit of output. As with the production budget, one solves for X, Y, and Z, sequentially:

X = 42,000*3 = 126,000 * 50% = 63,000 (based on the production needs for August)
Y = 108,000 + 63,000 = 171,000
Z = 171,000 – 54,000 = 117,000

Once the firm budgets for the quantity of each raw material, it would then budget for their acquisition costs, based upon the prices of the raw materials. Exhibit 6-1E presents RMI's **purchases budget** for July as follows:

Exhibit 6-1E
Purchases Budget (in dollars)

	July
Raw material purchases	117,000
* Standard cost per unit	$ 2.00
Cost of raw materials	$234,000

Realistically, multiple types of raw materials would compose an output. Therefore, management would set raw materials purchase budgets for the other inputs in a manner similar to those of Exhibits 6-1D and 6-1E.

Management next constructs a **cash budget** for July. This budget reflects expected cash receipts and disbursements for the month. RMI gathers the following information in addition to its raw materials purchase budget for cash budgeting purposes:

- Collects 80% of sales in the month of sale
- Collects the remaining 20% of sales in the month after the sale
- Pays for raw materials when purchased
- Incurs total operating expenses—$190,000
- Has noncash depreciation expense on administrative equipment—$12,000
- Pays for operating expense in the month incurred
- Pays for direct labor in the month incurred
- Pays for factory overhead in the month incurred
- Has an income tax rate of 40%
- Pays for income taxes in the month incurred

In order to simplify the budgeting illustration, we further assume that RMI must settle all of its factory overhead costs with cash. (Recall from Chapter 5 that numerous accounts offset actual factory overhead costs in addition to cash. For example, a firm would consume raw materials for the indirect materials portion of factory overhead, and accumulate depreciation for the cost apportionment of its factory equipment). Based on this assumption and ones bulleted above, Exhibit 6-1F presents RMI's cash budget for July.

Exhibit 6-1F
Cash Budget

Cash Receipts:		
Cash collections from July sales	$560,000	
Cash collections from June sales	100,000	
Total cash collections		$660,000
Cash Disbursements:		
Cash paid for purchases (Exhibit 6-5E)	234,000	
Cash paid for operating expenses ($190,000 – 12,000)	178,000	
Cash paid for direct labor (36,000 units * $4)	144,000	
Cash paid for factory overhead (36,000 units * $2)	72,000	
Cash paid for income taxes (per income statement below)	36,000	
Total cash payments		664,000
Net change in cash		($4,000)
Beginning cash balance—July 1, 2010		150,000
Forecast ending cash balance—July 31, 2010		$146,000

Firms sometimes must borrow on a short-term basis when projected cash balances fall below a minimum level set by management. In such cases, they account for those borrowings in their cash budgets. This is especially true for businesses that operate in highly seasonal industries.[6] Exhibit 6-1F implicitly assumes that $146,000 is an acceptable ending cash balance. Assume for the moment, however, that RMI deemed it must maintain a minimum cash balance of $150,000. The firm would need to secure a $4,000 short-term loan in July in order to meet this self-imposed standard. RMI would budget principal repayment and interest payments in future months that generate a cash surplus.

Master budgeting concludes with **pro forma financial statements**. These financial disclosures report an integrated set of forecast financial statements based on the budgets that compose the operating budget. Exhibit 6-2 draws on the information presented in Exhibits 6-1A through 6-1F to present the pro forma financial statements for RMI in July 2010.

Exhibit 6-2
Redlands Manufacturing, Inc.
Pro Forma Financial Statements

Forecast Income Statement—July 2010	
Sales revenues	$700,000
Cost of goods sold	420,000
Gross profit	280,000
Operating expenses	190,000
Pretax income	90,000
Income tax expense (40%)	36,000
Net income	**$ 54,000**

Forecast Retained Earnings Statement—July 2010	
Beginning retained earnings—July 1	$280,000
+ Net income	54,000
- Dividends	0
Ending retained earnings—July 31	**$334,000**

Forecast Balance Sheet—July 31, 2010				
Assets			**Liabilities**	
Cash	$146,000		Current liabilities	$0
Accounts receivable	140,000		Long-term liabilities	
Raw materials inventory (63,000 oz. * $2 per oz)	126,000		Bonds payable	270,000
Finished goods inventory (11,000 finished units * $12 per unit)	132,000			
Total current assets	544,000		**Shareholders' Equity**	
			Common stock	300,000
Equipment, net of depreciation	360,000		Retained earnings	334,000
Total assets	**$904,000**		**Total liabilities and s/ equity**	**$904,000**

Forecast Statement of Cash Flows—July 2010		
Net income	$54,000	
+ Depreciation expense	12,000	
- Increase in accounts receivable	(40,000)	
- Increase in raw materials inventory	(18,000)	
- Increase in finished goods inventory	(12,000)	
Cash flows from operating activities		(4,000)
Cash flows from investing activities		0
Cash flows from financing activities		0
Net change in cash		($4,000)
Beginning cash balance—July 1, 2010		150,000
Forecast ending cash balance—July 31, 2010		$146,000

COST-VOLUME-PROFIT ANALYSIS

Chapter 6 has thus far examined operating budgets with the objective of producing pro forma financial statements. This type of forecasting is important to projecting earnings, cash flows, and financial position. Managerial planning, however, extends beyond pro forma financial statements. Managers are interested in how the interrelationship between costs and sales affects profitability. Knowledge of such interactions enables management to alter assumptions about cost structure and pricing policies in order to forecast their effect on wealth creation. The remainder of this chapter examines this aspect of budgeting activity and the role of accounting in it.

Recall from Chapter 5 that one can separate cost behavior into fixed and variable components. This information proves beneficial in forecasting financial results. Managers realize that the total dollar amount of a *fixed cost* remains constant, regardless of an activity level, such as sales revenues or inventory production. Conversely, executives know that *variable costs* remain constant on a per unit basis. Consequently, changes in an activity either increase or decrease total variable costs.[7] Knowledge of these cost behaviors enables managers to rearrange disclosures and produce more informative income statements.

Many costs contain both fixed and variable cost components. An example of such a **mixed cost** is an electric utility cost. The service provider charges its consumers a flat monthly service fee plus a cost per kilowatt-hour.

Accountants use regression analysis to determine the fixed and variable cost portions of mixed costs.[8] For the sake of simplicity, we assume that the accounting function has separated all mixed costs into their fixed and variable components and identified them as such. The firm links these two types of cost behavior to sales activity in order to forecast profitability.[9]

GRAPHICAL ANALYSIS

Accountants refer to the overall process of relating costs to sales and profits as **cost-volume-profit (CVP) analysis**. The first step in understanding this process is through visual representation. Exhibit 6-3 presents a cost-volume-profit graph.

Exhibit 6-3
Cost-Volume-Profit Graph

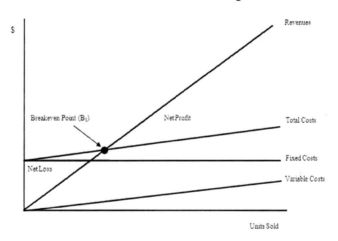

One notes that the total cost line sums the horizontal fixed cost line with the upward sloping variable cost line.[10] Inasmuch as revenues vary by activity (price * quantity), the revenue line is also upward sloping. Its slope, however, is steeper than that of the total cost line (the fixed cost line plus the variable cost line), because the retail selling price of a unit of inventory exceeds the purchase (or manufactured) cost of the good sold.

The intersection of total revenues and total costs defines the **breakeven point**. Exhibit 6-3 designates the breakeven point as B_1. The reader should note that the region above and to the right of B_1 reflects firm profitability. This profit region expands exponentially beyond the breakeven point because the firm has covered all of its fixed costs at B_1. The loss region exists to the right and below the breakeven point. The maximum loss amount equals the firm's fixed cost, or the intersection of the fixed cost line with the Y-axis. The firm generates no revenues at zero sales; however, it still incurs the full amount of fixed costs.

CVP Income Statements

As noted above, managers can rearrange the **income statement equation** based on cost behavior. They can rewrite the basic income statement equation as follows:

Sales revenues = fixed expenses + variable expenses + net income

Reflecting price and quantity factors, one expands this equation to the following:

Unit sales price * quantity sold = fixed expenses + (unit variable cost * quantity sold) + net income

A **contribution-margin income statement** more clearly demonstrates the income statement as a function of cost behavior than the above equations do. This type of income statement partitions costs into their variable and fixed components, instead of the classifications cost of goods sold and operating expenses. The name of the income statement derives from the concept of **contribution margin**, which is difference between revenue and variable cost on either a per unit or aggregate basis. Consider, for example, the Inland Empire Company's following GAAP-based income statement.

Sales revenues ($20 * 20 units)	$400
Cost of goods sold ($12 * 20 units)	<u>240</u>
Gross profit	160
Operating expense	<u>160</u>
Net income	$ 0

Assume that Inland Empire sold only one product at $20 per unit, and the firm's cost of goods sold varied in proportion to sales.[11] Fixed operating expenses were $120 and the remaining $40 of SG&A expenses varied with sales levels (a 10% or $2 per unit sales commission). We could rearrange the income statement as a contribution-margin income statement, and contrast it with the conventional one, as follows in Exhibit 6-4.

Exhibit 6-4
Inland Empire Company
Alternative Income Statements

Conventional (GAAP) Income Statement			Contribution Margin Income Statement	
Sales revenues ($20 * 20 units)	$400		Sales revenues ($20 * 20 units)	$400
Cost of goods sold ($12 * 20 units)	240		Variable cost of sales ($12 * 20 units)	240
Gross profit	160		Variable selling expenses ($2 * 20 units)	40
Operating expense ($40 + $120)	160		Contribution margin	120
Net income	$ 0		Fixed selling expenses	120
			Net income	$ 0

The reader should understand that both income statements report the same net income ($0 in this case), despite the alternative presentation of corporate expenses. In addition, while firms use contribution margin income statements extensively for profit planning purposes, generally accepted accounting principles do not allow this type of income statement presentation format for public disclosures.

Companies may also report their internal variable cost income statements on a contribution margin basis rather than in accordance with GAAP. Recall from Chapter 5 that variable-cost income statements do not capitalize the portion of fixed expenses related to unsold inventory. These types of income statements subtract the total amount of fixed costs from revenues, regardless of the sales level and inventoried items. We demonstrate this internal income statement approach by restating the Redlands example in Chapter 5. In that case, we assumed the following data:

Units produced	15
Sales	10 units @ $20
Variable product costs	$5 per unit
Fixed product costs	$60
Beginning inventory	0 units
Ending inventory	5 units

Exhibit 6-5 contrasts the two disclosure approaches as follows:

Exhibit 6-5
Redlands, Inc.
Alternative Variable Cost Income Statement Disclosures

Variable Costing Format		Contribution Margin Format	
Sales revenues ($20 * 10 units)	$200	Sales revenues ($10 * 20 units)	$200
Variable man. expense ($5 *10)	50	Variable cost of sales	50
Fixed manufacturing expense	60	Contribution margin	150
Gross profit	$ 90	Fixed selling expenses	60
		Gross profit	$ 90

BREAKEVEN CALCULATIONS

Managers use the relationship between cost behavior and revenue generation to evaluate future firm performance. One computes these expectations based on ratios resulting from algebraically rearranging the cost-behavior income statement equation.[12] We now explore CVP calculations beginning with breakeven computations, progressing through targeted income levels, and adjusting for income tax expenses. Along the way, we alter cost or revenue assumptions to demonstrate the effect that alternative inputs have on profitability.

One can calculate the breakeven point in either units sold or sales revenues. Using the data from Exhibit 6-4, we determine the per unit contribution margin as $6. This amount results by subtracting the sum of a $12 per unit variable cost of goods and the $2 per unit sales commission from the $20 per unit sales price. This knowledge allows us to compute the **breakeven point in units** as follows:

Fixed costs / unit contribution margin in dollars = breakeven point in units
$120 / $6 = 20 units

We can alter the breakeven point in unit's ratio in order to compute the **breakeven amount of sales revenues**. This adaption results in the following ratio:

Fixed costs / contribution margin ratio = breakeven point in dollars

One divides the unit contribution margin by the unit sales price to compute a **contribution margin ratio** (i.e., the denominator in the above equation). This produces a 30% contribution margin ratio ($6 / $20 = 30%) in this instance. Consequently, Redlands breakeven amount of sales revenues is $400:

$$\$120 / .30 = \$400$$

Note that the contribution-margin income statement in Exhibit 6-4 reflects the above breakeven amounts.

Managers often conduct **sensitivity analysis** by measuring the impact of alternative assumptions of the CVP data. Sensitivity analysis allows managers to determine numerous *what if* scenarios. For example, assume that Inland Empire's per unit variable cost of goods sold increased to $14 from $12. Due to competitive pressures in the industry, however, the firm could not pass along this cost to its customers. The firm would calculate its breakeven numbers under this scenario as follows:

Fixed expenses / contribution margin per unit = breakeven point in units
$120 / $4 = 30 units
Fixed expenses / contribution margin in percentage terms = breakeven point in revenue
$120 / .20 = $600

The contribution-margin income statement verifies the accuracy of these calculations:

Sales revenues ($20 * 30)	$600
Variable COGS ($14 * 30)	420
Variable sales comm. ($2 * 30)	60
Contribution margin	120
Fixed expenses	120
Net income	$ 0

One could conduct a further sensitivity analysis by changing revenue or fixed cost assumptions independently of, or in conjunction with, changes in the variable cost structure. For example, Inland Empire could contemplate reducing labor costs by automating some of its processes. This strategy would increase fixed costs and decrease variable ones. Sensitivity analysis would allow the firm to compare the breakeven point under the proposed shift in cost structure against that of the current cost composition. This information would assist management in deciding whether to automate the processes under consideration.

Profit Forecasts

The next step in CVP analysis is to calculate profitability. One treats targeted net income as another *fixed cost* in the CVP ratios. Using the original Exhibit 6-4 data, assume that the management of Inland Empire establishes a net income target of $30. This results in the following computations:

Sales in units: ($120 + $30) / $6 = 25 units
Sales revenues: ($120 + $30) / .30 = $500

Again, one uses the contribution-margin income statement to verify the calculations:

Sales revenues ($20 * 25)	$500
Variable COGS ($12 * 25)	300
Variable sales comm. ($2 * 25)	50
Contribution margin	150
Fixed expenses	120
Net income	$ 30

As with our discussion of breakeven analysis, a manager can employ sensitivity analysis to measure the effects of alternative assumptions. The firm might be interested in computing the sales level needed to reach a $30 profit target if it adjusts its pricing or cost structure. Assume for the moment that Inland Empire wants to generate a higher sales volume in order to increase market share. It decreases unit sales price by $1 in order to achieve this goal. The new sales price reduces unit contribution margin to $5 ($19 – [$12+ $2]). In order to reach $30 in profitability, the company must now sell 30 units ([$120 + $30] / $5).

Firms often express profitability as a percentage of sales rather than as a total dollar amount. In these instances, the manager first computes the desired **net profit margin** or **return on sales**. Net profit margin is the ratio of net income to sales revenues (i.e., net income / sales revenues). Next, the manager converts this return on sales percentage to a dollar amount. One then treats the dollar equivalent of the net profit margin as another *variable* cost in the cost-volume-profit equations.

Consider for example that Inland Empire targeted a net profit margin of 20% of sales. This 20% return on sales equals a unit profit of $4 ($20 selling price per unit *.20). Adding what is in effect another variable cost of $4 reduces the unit *contribution margin* to $2 ($20 – [$12+ $2 +$4]).[13] The revised *contribution margin ratio* is 10% ($20/ $2= 10%). This would yield the following CVP calculations:

Sales in units: $120 / $2 = 60 units
Sales revenues: $120 / .10 = $1,200

The contribution-margin income statement proves the accuracy of the above calculations:

Sales revenues ($20 * 60)	$1,200
Variable COGS ($12 * 60)	720
Variable sales comm. ($2 * 60)	120
Contribution margin	360
Fixed expenses	120
Net income	$ 240

We verify the 20% net profit margin by dividing net income by sales revenues or $240 / $1,200 = 20% net profit margin.

INCOME TAX CONSIDERATIONS

Income tax expense is a necessary cost of doing business; therefore, management must budget for the cost of taxes as they do for other operating expenses when analyzing cost, volume, and profit. The complicating factor in CVP analysis is that income tax expense is a variable cost that is a function of the amount of reported *pretax* income. Other variable expenses, as we have noted, move lockstep with sales revenues. Fortunately, managers can adjust profit levels to compensate for the derivative nature of the cost of income taxes. They do so by converting net income levels to their pretax basis. Business people refer to this technique as **grossing up net income**. One grosses up net income by dividing net income by one, minus the effective income tax rate. This pretax income then becomes the basis for the CVP calculations.

Assume the revenue and cost structure of Inland Empire in Exhibit 6-4, except that the firm is subject to a 40% income tax rate. If management targeted *net* income of $36 under this cost structure, it would first need to convert the $36 to its *pre-tax* equivalent of $60:

$$\$36 / (1 - .4) = \$36 / .6 = \$60$$

They would then treat pretax income as another fixed cost in determining sales levels or amounts for specific net income. The grossed-up net income becomes part of the basic calculation as follows:

Sales in units: ($120 + $60) / $6 = 30 units
Sales revenues: ($120 + $60) / .30 = $600

Sales revenues ($20 * 30)	$600
Variable COGS ($12 * 30)	360
Variable sales commissions ($2 * 30)	60
Contribution margin	180
Fixed expenses	120
Pretax income	60
Income tax expense (.40)	24
Net income	$ 36

Managers can also plan for specific levels of net profit margin if the firm is subject to income taxes. In this case, the manager grosses up the net profit margin to its pretax profit margin equivalent in *percentage* terms. He or she then converts the pretax profit margin to a dollar amount and treats that value as if it were another variable cost.[14] The following calculations demonstrate the process.

To illustrate the grossing up of a net profit margin, we assume the Exhibit 6-4 data with a 40% income tax rate and a net profit margin of 12%. The following calculations present the sales level and amount needed to insure a 12% net profit margin. The subsequent contribution-margin income statement validates the computations.

Pretax profit margin = .12 / (1 - .4) = .20 or 20%
Pretax profit per unit = $20 * .20 = $4.00
Therefore, the revised contribution margin is $2: $20 − ($12 + $2 + $4) = $2.
Sales in units: $120 / $2 = 60 units
Sales revenues: $120 / .10 = $1,200

Sales revenues ($20 * 60)	$1,200
Variable COGS ($12 * 60)	720
Variable sales comm. ($2 * 60)	120
Contribution margin	360
Fixed expenses	120
Pretax income	240
Income tax expense (.40)	96
Net income	$ 144

Note that the contribution-margin income statement above produces a *pretax* profit margin of 20% ($240 / 1,200) and a 12% *net* profit margin ($144 / $1,200).

MULTIPLE PRODUCTS ANALYSIS

The cost-volume-profit discussion thus far has centered on the analysis of a single product. Firms usually sell a variety of products, and each item has its own selling price and cost structure. As long as the sales mix remains relatively constant, cost-volume-profit analysis of more than one product is straightforward. The manager or accountant treats the sales mix as a unified basket of goods and analyzes cost, volume, and profit on that basis. One constructs a weighted-average contribution margin income statement under the basket approach, computes an overall activity level, and apportions the basket value on a relative sales basis.

Assume that Bulldog, Inc. provides the following per unit data for Products A and B, the two products it sells.

Product A		Product B	
Sales revenues	$10	Sales revenues	$ 5
Variable COGS	6	Variable COGS	3
Variable sales comm.	1	Variable sales comm.	.667
Contribution margin	$ 3	Contribution margin	$1.333

Further assume that the firm incurs $60 of fixed costs for Product A and fixed costs of $40 for Product B. The firm also sells 3 units of Product B for every 2 units of Product A. Exhibit 6-6A presents the company's revenue and cost structure:

Exhibit 6-6A
Basket Revenue and Cost Structure

	Product A (2 units)	Product B (3 units)	Basket of Goods
Sales revenues	$20	$15	$ 35
Variable COGS	12	9	21
Variable sales commissions	2	2	4
Contribution margin	6	4	10
Fixed costs	$60	$40	$100

The first step in multiple product CVP analysis is to compute the breakeven point for the basket of goods. The computations for Bulldog, Inc. are as follows:

Breakeven in units: $100 / $10 = 10 baskets
Breakeven in sales revenues: $100 / .2857 ($10/$35) = $350

The next step apportions the basket of sales to the respective products:
Product A: 10 baskets * 2 units per basket = 20 units
Product B: 10 baskets * 3 units per basket = 30 units

Exhibit 6-6B proves the accuracy of the above calculations:

Exhibit 6-6B
Basket Contribution Margin Income Statements

	Product A (20 units)	Product B (30 units)	Basket of Goods
Sales revenues	$200	$150	$350
Variable COGS	120	90	210
Variable sales commissions	20	20	40
Contribution margin	60	40	100
Fixed costs	60	40	100
Net income	$ 0	$ 0	$ 0

The manager could then extend the analysis by incorporating profit levels and income tax rates into the computation.

Summary

This chapter explored the relationship among managers, budgeting, and accounting. Accountants quantify the financial projections they receive from managers and produce forward-looking reports that assist in enterprise planning and control. A critical aspect of budgeting is the compilation of the master budget. This comprehensive budget enumerates operating activities for the next fiscal year. A master budget begins with a sales forecast and culminates in pro forma financial statements. The intermediate components of a master budget depend on business type—manufacturer, retailer, or service provider. Chapter 6 examined how a manufacturing entity focused considerable attention on the production and purchases aspects of its master budget. A critical feature of all master budgets, regardless of business type, is the projection of cash flows. This document budgets the expected amount and timing of cash receipts and disbursements, and by doing so, identifies the potential need for short-term financing.

Cost-volume-profit analysis composes the second budgeting aspect covered in this chapter, explaining how managers compute the breakeven point for a product in units and sales revenues. The next step addressed how managers can target profits on both a dollar basis and in terms of net profit margin. Managers must budget for expected income taxes as well as operating costs. This chapter demonstrated how to adjust the cost-volume-profit equations and ratios in order to account for the cost of income taxes. The final aspect of the CVP discussion centered on the accounting for multiple products offered by an entity. Managers use a composite approach for CVP analysis for their product mix; they then reapportion that composite CVP data to the specific products offered by the firm.

Key Terms

Breakeven amount in sales revenues
Breakeven point in units
Budgets
Capital budgets
Contribution margin
Contribution-margin income statement
Cost-volume-profit analysis (CVP analysis)
Cyclicality
Decomposition
Exponential smoothing
Grossing-up net income
Income statement equation
Judgmental sales forecasts
Linear regression analysis
Master budgets
Operating budgets
Pro forma financial statements
Randomness
Seasonality
Sensitivity analysis
Trend analysis

Assignments

Accounting Concepts Crossword

Across

[1] Per unit profit beyond the breakeven point, or the difference between revenue and variable cost per unit.

[2] Financial statements that forecast expected sales, expenses, profits, and other financial data for a future accounting period.

[3] A cost that contains elements of both fixed and variable behavior.

[4] This budget sets forth the units expected to be manufactured to satisfy budgeted sales and inventory requirements.

[5] Managers use this type of analysis to measure the affect of alternative assumptions on the CVP data.

Down

[1] These budgets focus on quantifying the near term expectations of the firm's core or central business activities.

[2] This budget presents an estimation of the cash inflows and outflows for a business.

[3] This budget typically extends beyond one year and revolves around the financing and investing activities necessary for sustainable business operations.

[4] The intersection of total revenues and total costs.

[5] The vital first-step in the budgeting process. This budget presents the estimated amount of anticipatedsales allocated by product, territory, or person.

DISCUSSION ITEMS

What Would Your Accountant Say?

A good manager adheres to sound budgeting principles in order to meet the organization's mission effectively, efficiently, and productively. Your company has decided to revamp its current budgeting process, and the president, knowing you are in the process of completing your MBA, has invited you to spearhead the project. He asks you to explain some of the more prevalent aspects of good budgeting. What would your accountant say to the president?

Theory vs. Practice

In theory, the "Master Budget" of a manufacturing firm should include the following components: (1) sales budget, (2) production budget, (3) purchases budget, (4) cash budget, and (5) pro forma financial statements. In practice, however, many companies do not use a formal budgeting process as part of their financial planning, or they skip some of the steps outlined in the chapter. Describe the budgeting process used at your current place of employment, or if none, at organizations where you previously worked.

PROBLEMS

Problem 6-1

CMC, Inc. forecasts the following sales for the second quarter of 2009, as well as actual March sales:

March (actual)	April	May	June	Second Quarter Total
$35,000	$40,000	$55,000	$60,000	$155,000

In addition:
  a. The company makes 60% cash sales.
  b. It collects credit sales in the month after the sale, except for 2% that are bad debts never realized in cash.
  c. CMC adjusts for its bad debts quarterly; therefore, it has no allowance for uncollectible accounts as of March 31, 2009.
  d. The firm budgets $48,000 for monthly operating expenses. That amount includes $4,000 for depreciation.
  e. CMC pays 70% of its expenses in the month incurred and the remaining 30% in the next month.

   f. CMC has $5,400 of cash at March 31, 2009, and it maintains a minimum $4,000 cash balance at the end of every month in order to ensure liquidity.

   g. The company has a line of credit with its bank that allows borrowing in $1,000 increments at 12% interest. All borrowing takes place *at the beginning* of the month in which the company requires cash.

   h. The company must repay the maximum possible principal in thousand dollar increments.

   i. The credit facility requires CMC to repay accrued interest to date whenever it repays principal.

   j. CMC must make principal repayments and interest payments at month's end (funds permitting).

Required:

Develop a cash budget (receipts, payments, and financing) for the second quarter of 2009.

Problem 6-2

Redlands Air, Inc. charges $75 per hour for flight instruction. The company has $25,000 of annual fixed administrative costs, and pays $15,000 rental expense to Inland Empire Airport each year. Redlands incurs a $20,000 annual insurance premium to insure its aircraft and facilities.

In addition, the company gathers the following variable cost data per hour of flight instruction:

- Instructor's salary $30
- Fuel   12
- Aircraft maintenance   6

Required:

A. Assume Redlands Air, Inc. does not have to pay income taxes due to previous years operating losses.

   1. Compute Redlands Air's breakeven point in *hours* of flight instruction (round up to the next whole hour).

   2. Determine the amount of *revenue* it needs to breakeven.

   3. Calculate the number of flight hours and the amount of revenue the firm needs in order to generate income of $40,000.

   4. Calculate the number of flight hours and the amount of revenue the firm needs in order to generate a 10% net profit margin (net profit margin = net income / sales revenues).

B. Answer the questions 1 through 4 in part A above if Redlands Air has a 40% income tax rate.

CASE 6-1

You are the Chief Financial Officer (CFO) for Zen Distributors, Inc. a media broker that secures shelf space in independent bookstores for small publishing companies. As a member of the company's executive team, you are preparing the operating budget for the fourth quarter of 2009. Your intent is to summarize the budget for team members and provide them with detailed schedules that support your overview.

Zen's general ledger provides you with current account data on September 30, 2009 (the end of the third quarter) of operations:

Accounts (account amounts in thousands of dollars)	Debit	Credit
Cash	$8,000	
Accounts receivable	20,000	
Inventory	36,000	
Buildings and equipment, net of depreciation	120,000	
Accounts payable		$21,750
Common stock		150,000
Retained earnings		12,250
Totals	$184,000	$184,000

Jack Closer, vice president of sales, estimated that sales should increase slightly from their fourth quarter levels of the previous year. Per your request, he forwarded his monthly fourth quarter sales estimates to you, along with the current month's actual sales and his forecast for January 2010.

Month	Sales
September (actual)	$50,000
October	60,000
November	72,000
December	90,000
January 2010	48,000

You next met with Mary Balance, Zen's controller. Ms. Balance informed you that the company prices its products in order to ensure a 25% gross profit margin on sales. Zen has met that margin throughout the first three quarters of 2009, and she was confident that the firm would meet this target margin in the near term. Mary also told you that, on average, 60% of Zen's customers pay in cash. Those customers receive a 1% discount on the invoice price. The remaining 40% of the customers pay on account.

Credit sales terms are n/2EOM. This means credit customers must pay the full invoice price by the end of the month following the month in which they purchased merchandise. Mary explained, "Our customers are pretty sophisticated, and they constantly manage their cash flows just as we do. Consequently, if we make a credit sale in October, they will pay us by the end of November."

Mary also stated that Zen typically writes off 1% of credit customer accounts as uncollectible. She added that despite this policy, no write offs were currently pending as of September 30 and none were expected to originate from third quarter activity. She stated, "In other words, we have a clean slate for the fourth quarter budget. We will collect all of the $20,000 accounts receivable balance at September 30 by the end of October. Therefore, bad debt expense and the allowance for doubtful accounts have zero balances at September 30, and we need to reestablish them for fourth quarter bad debts. We will write off 2009 fourth quarter bad debts sometime during 2010."

Mary also provided you with third quarter monthly expense data to assist in constructing your budget. The next table presents that information:

Monthly Expense Item	Amount
Administration	$2,500
General	6% of sales
Commissions	12% of sales
Depreciation	$850

She concluded, "As you know, we pay our operating expenses in the month we accrue them."

Procurement officer Jim Washburn managed inventory so that its ending balance equaled 80% of the next month's cost of goods sold. He also stated that the accounts payable clerk pays one half of each month's inventory cost in the month of acquisition, and the remaining 50% in the following month.

Ashleigh McNamara, head of minor asset acquisitions, informed you that Zen will make a cash purchase of $1,500 worth of handheld scanning devices in early October. Per corporate policy, the firm will depreciate this equipment over thirty months on a straight-line basis. Ashleigh added, "They'll be useless at the end of that time, so we will scrap them."

In your role as CFO, you insist that Zen maintain an ending monthly cash balance of $4,000 in order to remain financially flexible. The company has an open line of credit with its banking partner to ensure that it can meet its cash balance goal. This agreement mandates a 12% annual interest rate for all short-term borrowings. Financing must take place *at the beginning* of the month in thousand dollar multiples. Repayments of borrowing must also occur in thousand dollar increments, and the bank only accepts interest payments when Zen repays principal.

Required:

Compose a memorandum to Zen's management team that highlights the key aspects of the 2009 fourth quarter operating budget. Supplement your summary with budgetary schedules and attach them to the executive summary. The budgetary flow that you select is as follows:

- Cash collections
- Inventory purchases
- Cash disbursements for purchases
- Cash disbursements for operating expenses
- Overall cash budget (collections, disbursements, and financing)

You construct each of the above budgets on a monthly and quarterly basis. You may find it beneficial to construct your budgetary schedules in the manner presented in this chapter.

Finally, you conclude your budgets with a projected (pro forma) income statement for the fourth quarter and a pro forma balance sheet as of December 31. The company has a zero percent income tax rate, due to previous tax losses.

Endnotes

1   Once again, this statement assumes a for-profit entity.

2   One complexity is the effect of time on monetary values, which we introduced in Chapter 4. You will address this issue extensively in the finance course and that course will examine capital budgets.

3   Chapter 7 of this text examines variance analysis.

4   The reader should note that a retail firm does not have to budget for production, and it purchases inventory in its finished state from vendors. Service organizations have no need to budget for either production or inventory acquisitions.

5   Our budgetary discussions focus on a single item and its quantity to ease understanding.

6   Retailers, for example, have large cash outlays in the third fiscal quarter as they gear up for the holiday season. Many firms have to borrow short-term in order to maintain positive cash balances. These merchants repay the borrowing in the fourth quarter when holiday sales generate substantial cash flow.

7   As noted is Chapter 5, this discussion assumes certain simplifying assumptions such as fixed costs existing within a relevant range of activity and the linearity of all variable costs.

8   This process regresses total cost against total activity. The resulting Y-intercept equals the fixed cost and the slope of the regression line approximates the variable unit cost.

9   We define activity on a revenue basis for the purpose of this discussion. One can also define activity based on units produced rather than sold.

10   The generic terms for the economic sacrifice and their related economic sacrifice lines are *cost* and *cost* lines. When matched against revenues, the correct term is *expense* line. We use the term cost (or cost line) throughout our discussion because it is more prevalent in business usage.

11   Not all cost of goods sold are variable costs for a manufacturer. Depreciation on manufacturing facilities and equipment as well as property taxes on factories exemplify fixed product costs.

12   This text excludes the algebraic calculations. The interested reader can find them in cost accounting texts.

13   One can conceive of the net profit margin as a further reduction in contribution margin for the sake of computing breakeven points and target profit levels. Technically, the term contribution margin is inaccurate because the contribution margin, by definition, is sales revenue less variable costs, and a return on sales is not a variable cost.

14   This approach works as long as the dollar amount of the contribution margin remains a positive number. When the contribution margin equals $0 or less, one must address profit margin calculations on a marginal basis (above the breakeven point). This marginal approach exceeds the scope of this text.

Chapter 7

Control and Evaluation

CHAPTER LEARNING OBJECTIVES

Upon completion of this chapter, readers should be able to:
- ➢ Measure direct material, direct labor, and factory overhead variances.
- ➢ Distinguish between favorable and unfavorable variances.
- ➢ Analyze price, quantity, and total deviations from production standards.
- ➢ Evaluate managerial performance based on profitability, asset turnover, and return on assets.
- ➢ Apply the residual income concept to align divisional performance with corporate objectives.

This chapter focuses on the accounting system's contributions to managerial control. The previous chapter examined how accounting data helped managers plan performance by demonstrating the master budgeting process and targeting profit levels. Accounting information also enables managers to determine the extent to which anticipated results coincided with actual performance. This data allows managers to take corrective action as necessary, adjust future budgets when needed, and compensate individuals for their performance.

Two main areas compose Chapter 7: control and evaluation. First, we examine the need to contrast budgeted expectations with actual performance results. This portion of the chapter investigates the role that financial data play in controlling operations. The accounting system helps managers identify and correct deviations from expected results. Accounting for such operating variances enables managers to control current business processes and to improve future budgets. The second half of this chapter focuses on evaluating managerial performance. Accountants calculate financial metrics that assist in this task, and we explore their benefits and discuss their limitations.

CONTROL

An entity that carefully constructs budgets should expect results that mirror forecasts. A firm's operations are in control to the extent that they do, but significant budgetary departures signal a lack of control. Control exists along a continuum, rather that subsisting as in-control or out-of-control modes. Managers must judge when departures from expected values exceed tolerable limits. Critical challenges facing management include:

- reassessing the validity of budgets
- setting acceptable control limits
- investigating those events that depart from those limits
- correcting deviations when the benefits outweigh the costs of doing so

The accounting system provides key financial information for control-related decisions. Accountants measure performance, identify budgetary variances, and communicate findings to management. Managers then decide on the need for specific remediation. If the firm deems that corrective action is necessary, managers then determine the amount and timing of resources necessary to bring the process back into control.[1] Befitting an accounting text, this chapter focuses on financially measuring performance, and not on correcting deviations from the budget.

Accountants measure the differences between all of the elements of the master budget and their related results. Some departures within a master budget, however, are more critical than other variances. The productive processes used by the firm to create wealth (or meet its mission) compose the essence of firm operations. Accountants must measure, and managers must control, deviations from these critical aspects of the business. We can best understand this within the context of a manufacturing organization. The remainder of the first section of Chapter 7 examines the measurement of variances for direct materials, direct labor, and factory overhead.

VARIANCE ANALYSIS

Accountants define the difference between a budgeted monetary value and its actual dollar amount as a **variance**. Therefore, **variance analysis** is the systematic measurement, identification, explanation, and correction of budgetary deviations. We now calculate variances and analyze their meaning for direct materials, direct labor, and factory overhead in a hypothetical firm. A series of related exhibits presents budget, actual, and variance data for Redlands Containers, Inc. (RCI) a manufacturer of industrial-size plastic storage containers.[2]

The cost accountant of RCI summarizes the manufacturing standards and actual results for the company's most recent operating period in Exhibit 7-1A:

Exhibit 7-1A
Redlands Containers, Inc.
Budgetary and Actual Data

Direct Material and Direct Labor Standards for Each Container:
- 4 lbs. of plastic per container @ $3 per lb
- 3 hours of direct labor per container @ $5 per hour

Overhead Standards (based on machine hours):

Estimated total machine hours	20 hours
Machine hours per container	2 machine hours
Budgeted variable overhead costs	$20
Budgeted fixed overhead costs	$40

Actual Results:

Containers manufactured	12 containers
Total variable overhead costs	$32
Total fixed overhead costs	$42
Total direct materials used	40 lbs.
Cost per lb. of plastic	$2
Total direct labor hours	60 hours
Labor rate per hour	$6
Machine hours per container	2.5 hours

One must consider two critical factors before calculating variances. First, RCI determines its expected production run. Note from the data in Exhibit 7-1A that RCI applies factory overhead based on two (2) machine hours per container and the company expects to work 20 machine hours. Consequently, the firm has budgeted for the production of 10 containers during the accounting period (20 / 2 = 10 containers). This expected level of production determines the amount of factory overhead the firm *applies* to each unit of production.

Factory overhead applied can be computed on either an input or output basis. RCI budgets $20 for variable factory overhead, according to Exhibit 7-1A. From an input perspective, the company applies variable factory overhead at the rate of $1 per machine hour ($20 / 20 expected machine hours). Viewed as a function of output, the firm applies variable factory overhead at the rate of $2 per container ($20 / 10 containers). Although fixed factory overhead costs will not change regardless of the production level, RCI must still apply fixed factory overhead costs to each container it manufactures. The application rates for fixed factory overhead costs are as follows: $2 per machine hour on an input basis ($40 / 20 machine hours), and $4 per container on an output basis ($40 / 10 containers).[3]

The second critical aspect to understand is that actual production often does not equal the expected level. Exhibit 7-1A reports that the firm actually made 12 containers rather than the 10 that it forecasted. In other words, RCI produced two more plastic containers than anticipated. When calculating the budgets for materials, labor, and overhead, one multiples the standard unit quantity by the *actual* level of production (12 containers in this case) and not the budgeted level (10 containers). The completion of this example will demonstrate the importance of determining the correct overhead rate and setting standards based on actual production.

The accountant computes price, quantity, and total variances for each of the four key items in manufacturing. Sequentially, one computes variances for direct materials, direct labor, variable factory overhead, and fixed factory overhead. The most direct approach is to set up three data columns that contain budgetary, actual, and hybrid data. The left column in this three-column approach contains the actual results of operation. The right-hand column reports budgetary standards. The middle column determines cost based on actual quantity and standard (budgeted) costs. Variances are the difference between the column amounts. The following table presents the variances for direct materials:

Exhibit 7-1B
Direct Materials Variances

Actual Quantity * Actual Price		Actual Quantity * Standard Price		Standard Quantity * Standard Price
40 lbs. * $2 per lb.		40 lbs. * $3 per lb.		(4 lbs * 12 cont.) * $3 per lb.
$80		$120		$144
Direct materials price variance: $80 - $120 = $40 Favorable (F.)			Direct materials quantity variance: $120 - $144 = $24 Favorable (F.)	
Total direct materials variance: $80 - $144 = $64 Favorable (F.) ($40 F. price variance + $24 F. quantity variance = $64 F.)				

One precisely reads the topmost term in the right column of Exhibit 7-1B, designated as **Standard Quantity,** as *the standard quantity allowed for actual level of production.* Note that you multiply the standard materials for one plastic container (4 lbs. of plastic) by the actual number of containers made (12), and not the number the firm expected to make (10).

The **direct materials price variance** of $40 is the result of the difference between the actual cost of materials and actual quantity multiplied by the standard price per pound. (This is the absolute difference between $80 and $120.) The price variance is favorable (F.) because the actual price per pound ($2) is $1 less than the expected price of a pound of direct material ($3). You determine the $24 F. **direct materials quantity variance** in similar fashion. One can either add the two favorable variances together ($40 F. price variance + $24 F. quantity variance) in order to determine the **total direct materials variance** of $64 F., or you can measure the difference between actual material costs of $80 and standard material costs of $144. Again, the $64 direct materials variance is favorable because actual costs were less than budgeted ones.

Exhibit 7-1C presents variance computations for direct labor. These calculations mirror those for direct materials. Managers sometimes refer to the labor variances as rate and efficiency variances, instead of price and quantity variances. The following table presents the direct labor variance calculations.

Exhibit 7-1C
Direct Labor Variances

Actual Quantity * Actual Rate (Price)		Actual Quantity * Standard Rate (Price)		Standard Quantity * Standard Rate (Price)
60 hours * $6 per hour		60 hours * $5 per hour		(3 hrs. * 12 cont.) * $5 per hr.
$360		$300		$180
Direct labor rate (price) variance: $360 - $300 = $60 Unfavorable (U.)		Direct labor efficiency (quantity) variance: $300 - $180 = $120 Unfavorable (U.)		
Total direct labor variance: $360 - $180 = $180 Unfavorable (U.) ($60 U. rate variance + $120 U. efficiency variance = $180 U.)				

Notice the interchangeable terminology for direct labor variances, either labor *rate* or the *price* of labor. This results in a **direct labor rate (price) variance.** Similarly, a firm can be either efficient or inefficient with respect to the quantity of direct labor that it uses during production.[4] This **direct**

labor efficiency (quantity) variance, when coupled with the direct labor rate variance, yields a **total direct labor variance**.

Note that Exhibit 7-1C mirrors Exhibit 7-1B except for the numerical differences and the direction of the variances. Whereas RCI generated favorable direct material variances, those for direct labor were unfavorable. One could speculate the reason for these opposing variance results is that RCI reduced both the quality and quantity of direct materials actually used in the production process. (Note that both the costs and amounts of actual direct materials were less than the budgeted costs and amounts.) Conversely, actual direct labor costs and amounts exceeded their standards. In could be that RCI's use of inferior direct materials required greater direct labor efforts to convert the materials into finished products.

Factory overhead variances present the greatest measurement challenge to accountants and managers. Although deviations between expected and actual costs for direct materials and direct labor do occur, these measurements are straightforward as demonstrated in Exhibits 7-1B and 7-1C. More difficult, however, is the computation and interpretation of factory overhead variances. Recall from Chapters 5 and 6 that manufacturers *apply* overhead to production because they cannot accurately determine the actual amount of overhead to attach to each unit (and each job) during the production process. Consequently, factory overhead applied may differ from actual overhead because of numerous reasons, such as:

- the firm did not apply the proper overhead driver (or drivers) when computing the overhead applied rate
- the amount of budgeted overhead was unrealistic for the actual level of production
- specific actual overhead costs differed from their specific budgeted overhead costs counterpart (e.g., actual indirect labor costs differed from budgeted indirect labor costs)
- the process produced a different number of units than the firm budgeted for in the production run
- the firm ran a different number of jobs during the accounting period than it had budgeted for the period

Compounding these issues surrounding factory overhead variances is the fact that some overhead costs vary with production, while others remain fixed for all levels of productivity. For example, indirect materials and indirect labor are variable factory overhead costs. Depreciation and property taxes on manufacturing facilities are examples of fixed factory overhead costs. Exhibit

7-1D illustrates variable factory overhead variance measurements, and Exhibit 7-1E demonstrates fixed factory overhead measures.

Exhibit 7-1D
Variable Factory Overhead Variances

Actual Variable Overhead		Actual Quantity * Standard Rate (Price)		Standard Quantity * Standard Rate (Price)
Given in Exhibit 6-1A		(2.5 M.H. * 12 containers) * $1 M.H.		(2 M.H. * 12 containers) * $1 M.H.
$32		$30		$24
Variable factory overhead spending variance: $32 - $30 = $2 Unfavorable (U.)		Variable factory overhead efficiency variance: $30 - $24 = $6 Unfavorable (U.)		
Total variable factory overhead variance: $32 - $24 = $8 Unfavorable (U.) ($2 U. spending variance + $6 U. efficiency variance = $8 U.)				

Exhibit 7-1D reports that both variable factory overhead variances were unfavorable. The **variable factory overhead spending variance** was unfavorable because RCI spent $32 on factory overhead when it should have spend $30 based on the actual machine hours worked, actual containers produced, and standard variable factory overhead applied per machine hour.

Note that RCI also reported an unfavorable **variable factory overhead efficiency variance**. One attributes this unfavorable variance to the fact that the company worked 2.5 machine hours for each container that it manufactured and the standard called for only two (2) machine hours per container. The accountant determined that the standard application rate for variable overhead was $1 per machine hour because the budget called for $20 of variable overhead, and Redlands expected to work 20 machine hours. (Recall that the firm budgeted two (2) machine hours per container or 20 machine hours / 10 containers). RCI actually worked 2.5 machine hours on each unit; consequently, the firm was inefficient with its machine usage. This results in a $6 unfavorable variable factory overhead efficiency variance.

RCI's **total variable factory overhead variance** of $8 is the sum of the variable factory overhead spending and efficiency variances, or the difference between the actual variable factory overhead costs ($32) and the standard overhead cost allowed for 12 units of production ($24).

Exhibit 7-1E
Fixed Factory Overhead Variances

Actual Fixed Overhead		Budgeted Fixed Overhead		Standard Quantity * Standard Rate (Price)
Given in Exhibit 6-1A (actual results)		Given in Exhibit 6-1A (overhead standards)		(2 M.H. * 12 containers) * $2 M.H.
$42		$40		$48
Fixed factory overhead spending variance: $42 - $40 = $2 Unfavorable (U.)		Fixed factory overhead volume variance: $40 - $48 = $8 Favorable (F.)		
Total fixed factory overhead variance: $42 - $48 = $6 Favorable (F.) ($2 U. spending variance + $8 F. volume variance = $6 F.)				

The accountant treats the standards (right) column for fixed overhead on a *variable* cost basis. One takes this counterintuitive approach because the firm must apply a portion of the fixed overhead to each plastic container as it goes through the production process.[5] Note that the budgeted and actual fixed factory overhead cost data disclosed by RCI in exhibit 7-1A yield the cost amounts in both the left and middle columns of Exhibit 7-1E. The left column reports actual fixed factory overhead costs of $42, and the middle column reports the budgeted fixed amount of $40. The $40 middle column is not surprising because fixed costs do not relate to production levels, although one treats them as such for purposes of applying fixed factory overhead (the right column).

Exhibit 7-1E applies fixed overhead at $2 per machine hour ($40 budgeted fixed overhead / 20 machine hours). Consequently, RCI's manufacturing process yields an $8 F. **fixed factory overhead volume variance** because the company produced two (2) more containers (12) than it budgeted for (10 containers). In other words, Redlands spread its fixed overhead charges over two (2) more units of production than called for in the budget. This excess production created a favorable volume variance. The **fixed factory overhead spending variance** ($2 unfavorable) occurred because the firm's actual fixed overhead costs exceeded its budgeted costs for fixed factory overhead. As with the preceding three variances, one computes **total fixed factory overhead variances** in one of two ways: either as the difference between actual and applied fixed factory overhead costs, or as the sum of fixed factory overhead's spending and volume variances.

ADDITIONAL VARIANCE FACTORS

We end this section on variance analysis with three concluding notes:

1. *No* variance is the ideal result for any process. A zero variance is superior to a favorable variance because it reflects the matching of anticipated costs with actual costs. The term favorable only means that actual prices or quantities were less than forecast ones. While this may be a better result than cost overruns (unfavorable variances), it still connotes either budgeting inaccuracies or process inefficiencies. Therefore, a manager should not consider a favorable budget variance as a *good* result.

2. The firm must include all costs for material, labor, and overhead when setting standards. For example, direct material costs would include sales taxes and delivery charges. Direct labor costs include fringe benefits, such as medical coverage and pension benefits.

3. The entity accounts for direct labor overtime costs (the *additional* hourly wage rate) as a variable overhead cost. It does not account for these overtime premiums as a direct labor cost. One accounts for direct labor overtime costs in this manner because overtime costs apply to all production jobs, and not just the jobs that occur toward the end of a production cycle.

The ability of managers to set and meet accurate budgets indicates good managerial performance. Performance failure signals ineffective management. The organization should reward the former and punish the later. The remainder of Chapter 7 examines prominent performance evaluation methods.

PERFORMANCE EVALUATION

Managers operate in one of three types of environments: cost, profit, and investment centers. Regardless of structure, the firm holds managers accountable for their results, and the accounting function calculates the financial metrics needed for evaluation. The manager of a **cost center** can only control the costs associated with his or her operations. Consequently, the firm rates managerial performance based upon one's ability to minimize costs. An entity judges managers of **profit centers** on income generation. The **investment center** concept evaluates results based on the relationship between operating earnings and the resources committed to those operations. Investment centers are the best way to measure managerial results because they consider the inputs (investments or assets) required to produce outputs (income). The following discussion of performance evaluation focuses on the investment center concept.

RETURN ON ASSETS

Managers use their resources to create value for the firm. Asset utilization measures how well a manager generates earnings with the resources at his or her disposal. The first step in evaluating a manager's performance, therefore, is to measure an investment center's return on assets (ROA). This financial metric reports the percentage of income earned for each dollar invested in an entity's resources.[6] Recall from Chapter 3 that we compute ROA as follows:

Return on assets = operating income / [(beginning assets + ending assets) / 2]

The return on assets measure is the conventional means by which a firm evaluates managerial performance of its investment centers.[7] People more commonly refer to operating income, the numerator in the ratio, as **earnings before interest and taxation** or **EBIT**. While this measure conveys information about how well a manager creates wealth for the firm, it does have limitations that we will explore later in this section.

The firm can gather additional information about managerial performance by examining the ROA components. Asset returns result from interaction between operating profit margins and asset turnover. Profit margin is the proportion of income to revenues, and asset turnover equals revenues divided by total assets (averaged for the year). This measure reports the amount of sales each asset dollar generated in a given time period. One defines ROA in component form as follows:

Return on assets = operating profit margin * asset turnover

or

Net income / total assets = (operating income / revenues) * (revenues / total assets)

The reader should note that the revenue items in the profit margin's denominator and asset turnover's numerator cancel out, yielding the computation of an overall asset return as operating income divided by total assets.

Exhibit 7-2 demonstrates the return on asset results for two divisions within Inland Empire, Inc.

Exhibit 7-2
Inland Empire, Inc.
Return on Assets (in thousands)

Item	Division A	Division B	Total
Operating income	$10	$20	$30
Assets	80	220	300
Revenues	150	350	500
Return on assets (ROA)	12.5%	9.1%	10%
Operating profit margin	6.67%	5.71%	6%
Asset turnover	1.88 times	1.59 times	1.67 times

Although Division A generated only one half the amount of income as Division B ($10,000 versus $20,000), Division A produced a higher return on invested assets (12.5% versus 9.1%). Both a higher operating profit margin and greater asset turnover drove Division A's higher overall return on assets than that of Division B. The data indicate that the manager of Division A more efficiently used available assets to create wealth than did the manager of Division B.

Return on investment (assets) influences managerial decisions. The manager of a division will accept projects that offer a return on assets greater than the current ROA. For example, assume for the moment that the two divisions from Exhibit 7-2 each had the opportunity to invest in a project that offered an 11% return on investment. The manager of Division B would accept the project because its return would increase the current 9.1% return on investment earned by the division. Division A's manager, on the other hand would reject the investment because an 11% return would lower his or her current divisional return of 12.5%.

NET DEBT FINANCING

An entity could report on a divisional net income basis (i.e., earnings after interest and income tax expenses) instead of EBIT. A firm allocates a portion of its total borrowing and income tax expenses to each one of its divisions in determining divisional income. Embedded in this approach is the concept that each division should bear its share of these non-operating business costs. The ROA calculations under this method are the same as those discussed above, except that net income substitutes for operating income in the overall return on assets and profit margin ratios.

A problem with the net income approach exists, however, when the entity uses debt to finance additional investments. Recall from Chapter 3 that interest on borrowed funds shields a portion of revenues from taxation. This income tax deduction reduces the effective cost of borrowing to the amount of the interest expense multiplied by one, minus the income tax rate. Therefore, a firm that measures divisional earnings on a *net* income basis must use *net* interest expense when computing divisional returns on assets and determining whether to accept or reject divisional investment projects.

RESIDUAL INCOME

Using ROA to evaluate managerial performance may not serve the best interest of the firm as a whole. To understand why, we first revisit the weighted average cost of capital concept introduced in Chapter 4. As noted in that chapter, the assets that divisions deploy to earn income are not without cost. The cost of capital represents the economic sacrifice the firm makes to acquire wealth-creating investments. Companies compute their cost of capital as the weighted average sum of the cost of debt financing and the cost of equity financing. This equation, derived in Chapter 4, is as follows:

$$\text{WACC} = (\% \text{ of debt}) \text{ (net cost of debt)} + (\% \text{ of common stock}) \text{ (cost of common equity)}$$

The entity only creates wealth from an investment when its benefits (income) exceed its cost of funds (sacrifices). Consequently, the firm should invest in all projects whose earnings are greater than their *entity's* capital costs. This firm-wide decision rule, however, sometimes conflicts with the divisional approach of undertaking projects that yield a positive divisional return on assets. We will illustrate this conflict by continuing the evaluation of divisional performance of Inland Empire, Inc.

Assume that Inland Empire's weighted average cost of capital (for both debt and equity) was 10%, and that both divisions had the opportunity to invest $100,000 in a project with the previously assumed 11% rate of return on assets. As noted, if the firm evaluated managerial performance based on ROA, the Division A manager would reject the investment while the Division B manager would accept it. The decision of Division A, however, would not be in the best overall interest of Inland Empire. Fortunately, the firm can substitute a measure of residual income in place of ROA in order to improve managerial performance measurement.

Residual income is the net operating income that a *division* earns above the *firm's* cost of capital. Divisions accept all projects that exceed the firm's cost of capital, and reject those below it. Exhibit 7-3 demonstrates the advantage to Inland Empire if it measures divisional performance using a residual income approach.

Exhibit 7-3
ROA versus Residual Income
ROA Decision Rule
Pro Forma Return on Assets (in thousands)

Item	Division A (reject an 11% project)	Division B (accept an 11% project)	Total
Operating income	$10	$31 ($20 + 11)	$41
Assets	80	320 ($220 + $100)	400
ROA	12.5%	9.7%	10.25%

Residual Income Decision Rule
Pro Forma Results (in thousands)

Item	Division A (accept an 11% project)	Division B (accept an 11% project)	Total
Operating income	$21	$31 ($20 + $11)	$52
Assets	180 ($80 + $100)	320 ($220 + $100)	500
ROA	11.67%	9.7%	10.4%
Return on proposed investment	$11 (100 * .11)	$11 (100 * .11)	$22
Cost of capital	10 (100 * .10)	10 (100 * .10)	20
Residual income	$1	$1	$2

Exhibit 7-3 demonstrates that Inland Empire maximizes its overall return on investment when both divisions accept their investment opportunities (an ROA of 10.4% versus 10.25%). This result is obtained despite the lowering of Division A's ROA from 12.5% to 11.67%. The data indicate that divisions should accept all projects that exceed the firm's cost of capital because such projects increase *firm* ROA. Positive *divisional* residual income represents an increase in overall firm ROA. The upshot of the residual income approach is that the firm should establish incentives that reward creating residual income, even if an investment lowers a divisional manager's return on assets.

Many firms add precision to the residual income approach by adjusting their overall cost of capital for specific divisions. They do so because not all divisions within a firm are equivalent operating units. For example, Division

A of Inland Empire, Inc. may compete in a rapidly growing business segment, while Division B operates in a mature industry. Consequently, the two divisions have distinctly different investment opportunities, and their potential investments have different risk profiles. Inland Empire could establish specific minimum required return on asset levels for each of its divisions. Such rates represent the cutoff point, or a hurdle rate, that the division must surpass in order to accept an investment opportunity.

Assume for the moment that Inland Empire established a minimum return on assets rate of 12% for Division A and 9% for Division B. Both divisions again had the opportunity to invest in $100 (thousand) projects offering an 11% return on investment. In this case, the manager of Division A would reject the investment because it would yield negative residual income. Exhibit 7-4 presents the alternative decisions:

Exhibit 7-4
Department Residual Income
Pro Forma Results (in thousands)

Item	Division A (accept an 11% project)	Division B (accept an 11% project)	Total
Return on proposed investment	$11 (100 * .11)	$11 (100 * .11)	$22
Department cost of capital	$12 (100 * .12)	9 (100 * .09)	21
Residual income	($1)	$2	$1

Item	Division A (reject an 11% project)	Division B (accept an 11% project)	Total
Return on proposed investment	$0	$11 (100 * .11)	$11
Department cost of capital	$0	9 (100 * .09)	9
Residual income	$0	$2	$2

Exhibit 7-4 demonstrates that Inland Empire, Inc. maximizes its residual income when Division B accepts its investment opportunity, because the rate of return exceeds its hurdle rate. The 11% rate of return for the Division A project does not meet its 12% cutoff rate; therefore, the Division A manager would reject the investment opportunity.

Summary

Accounting information helps managers control and measure operating performance. Good control requires that actual results should reflect budgeted amounts. Sound managerial practice requires that the firm measure, investigate, and correct material variances from production standards. Chapter 7 demonstrated the analysis of variance in a manufacturing environment. It illustrated how an accountant measures deviations from production standards for direct materials, direct labor, and factory overhead. The measurement process divides total direct material, direct labor, and variable factory overhead variances analysis into price (rate) and quantity (efficiency or spending) deviations. One also computes fixed overhead costs. The unique treatment of applying a portion of budgeted fixed factory overhead costs to each unit produced creates a fixed overhead volume variance when actual production levels deviate from budgeted activity. Managers classify every variance from production standards as either a favorable or an unfavorable variance. No difference between actual and expected performance (a zero variance), however, is the optimal result; it represents an in-control system or process.

The second portion of this chapter evaluated managerial performance at both the divisional and corporate level. Return on assets (ROA), or operating income divided by total assets, is the conventional managerial performance measure. Firms divide ROA into its component measures: calculating both profit margin (operating income / revenues) and asset turnover (revenues / total assets) yields even greater insights about operating performance than using aggregate ROA as a performance indicator. An evaluator can use ROA to rank divisional performance within the organization. Return on assets also guides investment decisions: a manager should only invest in projects that will generate an expected rate of return in excess of current ROA. Lack of accountability for the cost of capital limits the value of ROA computations, and may be incompatible with the overall firm objective of maximizing wealth. The residual income measure includes the weighted average cost of capital in its performance assessments; consequently, it results in investment decisions that align with the overall corporate objectives.

Key Terms

Cost center
Direct labor efficiency (quantity) variance
Direct labor rate (price) variance
Direct materials quantity variance
Direct materials price variance
Earnings before interest and taxation (EBIT)
Fixed factory overhead spending variance
Fixed factory overhead volume variance
Investment center
Profit center
Residual income
Standard quantity
Total direct labor variance
Total direct materials variance
Total fixed factory overhead variances
Total variable factory overhead variance
Variable factory overhead efficiency variance
Variable factory overhead spending variance
Variance
Variance analysis

Assignments

Accounting Concepts Crossword

Across   **Down**

[1] Ratio that presents revenues divided by total assets (averaged for the year).

[2] Costs incurred in production other than the costs of direct materials and direct labor.

[3] The manager of this operation attempts to maximize earnings.

[4] Fixed overhead variance that occurs because actual fixed overhead costs exceed budgeted ones.

[5] The manager of this operation attempts to minimize costs.

[1] The systematic measurement, identification, explanation, and correction of budgetary deviations.

[2] Labor variance that represents the difference between the actual and standard quantity of hours multiplied by the standard price per hour.

[3] The proportion of income to revenues.

[4] Fixed overhead variance that occurs because actual production exceeds budgeted production.

[5] The net operating income that a division earns above the firm's cost of capital.

DISCUSSION ITEMS

What Would Your Accountant Say?

An organization holds its managers accountable for their results, and the accounting function calculates the financial metrics needed for performance evaluation. Two of the metrics used by your firm to assess managerial performance are return on assets (ROA) and residual income. A group of management trainees has asked you to explain how these indicators are used. What would your accountant say?

Theory vs. Practice

This chapter described the use of variance analysis in a manufacturing environment. In theory, you can apply variance analysis to any set of financial or operational results in order to support cause analysis and answer the question, "What caused this variance?" Describe how your organization uses variance analysis in practice to improve efficiency.

PROBLEMS

Problem 7-1

Badlands Container, Inc. expects to manufacture eight (8) containers. It presents it standard costs and actual costs for the production run:

Direct Materials and Direct Labor Standards for Each Container:
- 4 lbs. of plastic per container @ $4 per lb.
- 2 hours of direct labor per container @ $7 per hour.

Overhead Standards (based on direct labor hours):

Budgeted variable overhead costs	$48
Budgeted fixed overhead costs	$32

Actual Results:

Containers manufactured	7 containers
Total variable overhead costs	$43
Total fixed overhead costs	$29
Total direct materials used	32 lbs.
Cost per lb. of plastic	$5
Total direct labor hours	12 hours
Labor rate per hour	$6

Required:

Compute the following variances for Badlands Containers, Inc. Designate each variance as either favorable (F.) or unfavorable (U.).

a. Direct materials—price, quantity, and total direct materials variances

b. Direct labor—rate, efficiency, and total direct labor variances

c. Variable factory overhead—spending, efficiency, and total variable factory overhead variances

d. Fixed factory overhead—spending, volume, and total fixed factory overhead variances

Variable O/H.

$$\frac{\$48}{8 \text{ cont} \times 2 \text{ DL}} = \$3 \text{ Variable rate per DLH.}$$

Fixed O/H

$$\frac{\$32}{8 \text{ cont} \times 2 \text{ DHL}} = \$2 \text{ Applied Fixed O/H pro per. DLH.}$$

Problem 7-2

Redlands Institute offers training at four regional campuses. The organization treats each campus as an investment center and evaluates its managers accordingly. Redland's accountant gathers the following data for its campuses:

Item	Ontario	Riverside	Temecula	Burbank	Redlands
Assets—Jan. 1	$240,000	$390,000	$150,000	200,000	$980,000
Assets—Dec. 31	260,000	370,000	165,000	210,000	1,005,000
Sales revenues	500,000	600,000	225,000	390,000	1,715,000
Operating income	50,000	32,000	20,000	26,000	128,000
New investment cost	100,000	160,000	140,000	80,000	
Expected return on new inv.	12,000	21,600	21,700	6,400	
Firm cost of capital	10%	10%	10%	10%	
Divisional cost of capital	11%	7%	16%	9%	

Required: Complete each of the following tables:

a. Current ROA and its components based on EBIT (excluding new investment opportunity)

Item	Ontario	Riverside	Temecula	Burbank	Redlands
Operating profit margin					
Asset turnover					
ROA					

b. New Investment Opportunity--ROA based on EBIT (decision = accept or reject)

Item	Ontario	Riverside	Temecula	Burbank
ROA-%				
Decision				

c. Combined ROA based on EBIT*

Item	Ontario	Riverside	Temecula	Burbank	Redlands
Combined ROA					

* For *accepted* divisional projects—add the new investment income to the current operating income to determine the combined operating income (the ratio's numerator) and add the amount of the new investment to the

average assets to determine combined total assets (the ratio's denominator). Use the ROA excluding new investment opportunities for *rejected* divisional projects.

d. Residual income (EBIT)—firm cost of capital approach

	Ontario	Riverside	Temecula	Burbank	Redlands
Income from new investment					
Firm cost of capital on new investment					
Residual income (EBIT)					
Investment decision					
Redlands ROA	-----	-----	-----	-----	

e. Residual income (EBIT)—division cost of capital approach

	Ontario	Riverside	Temecula	Burbank	Redlands
Income from new investment					
Division cost of capital on new investment					
Residual income (EBIT)					
Investment decision					
Redlands ROA	-----	-----	-----	-----	

Case 7-1

Early American Replications, Inc. (EAR) reproduces classic colonial-period furniture. The chief executive officer senses that the company does not adequately control production costs. Her expertise, however, lies in marketing and sales. The head of production, on the other hand, is a talented artisan but numerically unsophisticated. EAR has hired you as corporate controller to assure quality accounting, including accurate product costs and variance analysis.

You immediately identify a major problem—Early American Replications lacks standard costs for all of its products! Rather than address this significant problem all at once, you design a pilot program that standardizes the cost of producing the Jeffersonian, which is the company's best-selling table. Your objectives are to:

- compute a theoretically valid and operationally viable standard cost for the table
- determine a flexible budgeting cost equation for it

- identify variances between expected performance and actual results
- apply knowledge gained from this pilot study to other products produced by the company

You learn from the shop's craftspeople that replicating the Jeffersonian table is a relatively straightforward manufacturing job. Production, however, requires substantial woodworking skills and is a highly labor-intensive process. Each table requires substantial direct labor hours to complete. Moreover, the firm does not use automated machinery when making its Jeffersonian tables.

Your next step is to gather what cost data currently exists pertaining to the table. You gather information from purchase orders and employee worksheets and compile the data as follows:

Direct Materials and Direct Labor Standards

8 board feet of oak @ $7 per foot (excluding shipping charges)
6 hours of direct labor per table @ $18 per hour (excluding benefits)

Your manufacturing overhead cost estimates for one production run are as follows:

Manufacturing Overhead Costs

Total direct labor hours	600 hours
Total machine hours	300 hours
Total manufacturing overhead (60% fixed and 40% variable)	$3,000

You conclude after observing plant operations and researching industry standards that a single cost driver (or activity base) is sufficient to allocate manufacturing overhead. The costs of implementing an activity-based cost accounting system outweigh the benefits at this time. In addition, conversations with various management personnel reveal the following:

- Corporate policy requires purchasing lumber as close to each production run as possible and only in amounts needed for that production run. In addition, the Jeffersonian requires a unique grade of oak than other products, and there are no alternative uses for the Jeffersonian oak. Management determines that the cost of storing any excess lumber inventory outweighs its benefits; therefore, they scrap any Jeffersonian oak that exists after production.

- The central store's manager confirms corporate policy by informing you that there was no inventory of Jeffersonian oak prior to this production run.
- The logistics head states that the company pays shipping charges to third party transporters for its purchased goods. EAR pays these costs, which equal 20% of the Jeffersonian oak's invoiced price, upon receipt of product. Shipping is a necessary cost of the materials because, as the logistics person said, "We can't work the wood unless we pay the freight."
- The human resources director states that every employee earns company pension, medical, and other fringe benefits equal to one third (33.3333%) of his or her actual hourly wage. EAR pays a 50% premium (time and a half) on overtime wages. The firm pays fringe benefits at the normal rate of one third of actual normal hourly wages. (In other words, it does not pay a fringe benefit premium on overtime wages.)
- The production manager informs you that the firm usually produces the Jeffersonian table after it makes its other products. Consequently, the employees often have to work overtime in order to produce those tables.

Early American's accounting records contain the following actual manufacturing costs for the
Jeffersonian table. After verifying their accuracy, you summarize the results below:

Actual Results

Tables manufactured	95 tables
Total fixed manufacturing overhead	$1,920
Total board feet of oak purchased	800 feet
Total board feet of oak used	720 feet
Cost per foot of oak (excluding shipping charges)	$6.90 per foot
Total machine hours	315 hours
Total direct labor hours (includes 50 hours of overtime)	665 hours
Labor rate per hour (excluding benefits)	$15
Total variable manufacturing overhead (excluding overtime premium)	$1,650

Your job now is to measure expected performance against actual results for the pilot study.

Required: Prepare a memo to the CEO, not to exceed two pages, on your findings that:
a. concludeswhether or not the overall process is in control
b. provide a plausible explanation for the direct labor rate and efficiency variances
c. assign responsibility to the variable overhead efficiency variance (select among the persons in charge of purchasing, direct labor, machine hours, or manufacturing overheard)
d. explain why the fixed overhead volume variance is either favorable or unfavorable.

To assist in this assignment, complete the three items presented on the following page. Include them as an attachment to your memorandum.

1. Determine the standard cost of each table by completing the following table.

Item	Amount
Direct (raw) materials	$
Direct labor	
Variable manufacturing overhead	
Fixed manufacturing overhead	
Standard cost per table	$

2. Flexible Budget for the Jeffersonian Table
Present the flexible budgeting equation for the Jeffersonian table's standard cost. (i.e., Total cost = Fixed cost + variable cost * X). Note that X represents a number of tables.

3. Record your variances in the following table.

Manufacturing Variances

Direct Materials	Price	Quantity	Total
Direct Labor	Rate	Efficiency	Total
Variable Manufacturing Overhead	Spending	Efficiency	Total
Fixed Manufacturing Overhead	Budget	Volume	Total

Endnotes

1   Good budgeting requires that management allocate resources for the eventuality that it will have to correct certain operating variances.

2   As with other examples in this text, we present data in overly simplified form (e.g., a single input for a single output) in order to focus on the implications of the data.

3   The computations related to fixed factory overhead variances later in the chapter (Exhibit 7-1E) will revisit and clarify the need to apply fixed factory overhead as though it was a variable cost.

4   A direct labor usage variance is another synonym for a direct labor efficiency or quantity variance.

5   A review of the job-order costing system journal entries in Chapter 5 will help reinforce this concept.

6   You may find it helpful to think of this ratio as ROTA: return on total assets.

7   We favor the term return on assets over the more generic return on investment (ROI) terminology, because the economic concept of investment pertains to equity (or net asset) investments as well as to total assets.

Appendix A

Financial Statement Analysis

This appendix presents techniques for analyzing financial statements. Managers who can rigorously analyze disclosures about financial performance, position, and cash flows will make good economic decisions. They can logically infer the financial implications among alternative operating, financing, and investing options, and choose the most advantageous.

A reporting entity presents both entity-wide and segmented financial statements. Good managers *can read the financials* at both the divisional and corporate levels. The firm publicly reports consolidated financial statements, but most managers are more concerned with the financial performance and position of their specific business segment or division. Regardless of the reporting unit, managers should divide financial statements into feasible segments in order to understand their information content. Chapter 7 of the text already addressed one aspect of financial statement analysis—asset utilization and returns on investment. Therefore, this appendix addresses three other important analytical areas:

1. operating performance
2. liquidity
3. capital structure

The remainder of this appendix addresses each of these three components. The numerical examples in this appendix reflect the Extreme Edge financial statements (Exhibit 2-1 of Chapter 2).

OPERATING PERFORMANCE

A manager analyzes operating performance in order to determine the extent to which an entity will generate sufficient and sustainable amounts of income in the future. Managers define earnings sufficiency as the amount of income necessary to maintain and grow the business. They consider earnings sustainability as the ability of a business to replicate earnings from one reporting period to the next. In other words, operating performance analysis concerns itself with determining whether an enterprise generates *enough* and the *right kind* of earnings. That determination forms the basis for what managers commonly refer to as earnings quality, or the ability of an entity to add shareholder value over time.

Earnings quality assessments result in large part from an interpretation of prior income statements and operating cash flows. A history of wealth creation and cash flows from central business activities bodes well for a firm. On the other hand, lack of achievement in these areas raises questions about corporate vitality, and perhaps, viability. Earnings and cash flows from non-core transactions also affect earnings quality, but to a far lesser extent than income earned from on-going business operations. Managers evaluate income statements to determine the relative wealth enhancements from these income components. They value core wealth-building activities, but discount the worth of peripheral events.

Managers constantly make judgments about earnings quality. This task continually challenges them. Managers must thoroughly understand the sources of revenues and expenses that produced income during the reporting period. After doing so, a manager can rate earnings quality on a continuum ranging from low to high quality. Earnings numbers that represent true economic value, as opposed to the appearance of it, have a relatively high earnings quality.

INCOME STATEMENT SECTIONS

A useful way of grasping earnings quality is to divide the income statement into two sections, as Exhibit A-1 demonstrates:

Exhibit A-1
Income Statement Composition

Operating Section	Non-Operating Section
Revenues	+/- Other revenues and expenses
- Cost of goods sold	= Income before income taxes and extraordinary items
= Gross margin	- Income tax expense
- Operating (S,G, and A) expenses	+/- gains and losses from extraordinary items (net of tax)
= Operating income	= Net income
	EPS

The operating section reports the difference between a company's primary sources of revenues and the costs required to produce them, and the non-operating section reports secondary economic events that changed wealth during the period reported. Thus, managers focus on the operating section of the income statement because it contains more information about earnings sufficiency and sustainability than earnings from non-core business events.

Income statements for individual business segments often only present an operating section. They may ignore the non-operating business events altogether. Operating disclosures focus management attention on how well each segment of the business has performed. These individual segmented income statements, however, overstate the earnings quality of the firm as a whole. The firm incurs organization-sustaining costs that lower replicable earnings. Such costs include general administrative expenses, financial charges on borrowed funds, and income taxes.

Analyzing Profit Margins

Managers should compute, trend, and benchmark the following income metrics:

- Gross profit margin (or gross margin)
- Operating profit margin
- Net profit margin (if applicable)

Managers refer to each of these common size income measures as a profit margin; these ratios specify an income level as a percentage of revenues. Gross profit margin, for example, is the proportion of gross profit to revenues. One computes operating profit margin by dividing sales into operating income. In addition, the manager finds it useful to compute the operating profit margin both before and after other revenues and expenses, such as interest income and expense. Finally, net income divided by revenues equals net profit margin.

The following exhibit summarizes the three profit margins for Extreme Edge in 2009.

Exhibit A-2
Extreme Edge
2009 Profit Margins

Profit Margin	Ratio	Computation
Gross profit margin	Gross profit / sales revenues	$540 / $1,200 = 45%
Operating profit margin	Operating income / sales revenues	$55 / $1,200 = 4.6%
Adjusted operating profit margin	Operating income after financial rev. and exp. / sales revenues	$35 / $1,200 = 2.9%
Net profit margin	Net income / sales revenues	$35 / $1,200 = 2.9%

Managers must assess profit margins carefully. They must forecast the probability of future events that could change income levels and their cash consequences. A manager should ask the following questions and similar queries:

1. How will competition and consumer demand affect sales?
2. How will such changes in sales affect fixed cost coverage?
3. What is the probability that vendors will raise product prices?
4. Can the firm pass increased supplier costs to its customers?
5. Will operating expenses increase, decrease, or stabilize in future reporting periods?
6. Can the company cut certain operating costs without reducing operations, alienating customers, or affecting product quality?

Responses to these and similar questions enable the manager to forecast future performance accurately. Consider questions three and four for the moment. Assume that Extreme Edge's suppliers will raise prices (question 3), but that the company will be unable to pass the price increases on to its customers (question 4). The firm's gross profit margin will decline, which will in turn reduce operating and net profit margins.

OPERATING PERFORMANCE MEASURES

The remainder of this section of the appendix examines operating performance ratios. It links operating cash flows to those from investing and financing activities, with the goal of generating insights about the firm's quality of earnings.

An entity must generate enough operating cash to compensate investors and maintain productive capabilities. Cash sufficiency measures quantify the extent to which the entity succeeds in meeting these objectives. Managers combine relative amounts of cash with other data to judge the firm's ability to meet its cash obligations. *Cash flow adequacy* is the primary measure of an enterprise's ability to establish or replenish its productive base and make distribution to owners. We compute this ratio as follows:

Cash flow adequacy = cash flows from operating activities / (fixed assets purchased + cash dividends distributed)

A ratio of one (or 100%) or more provides evidence that a firm's operating cash flows were sufficient to replace obsolete resources and compensate owners for their investment. A ratio of less than one has the opposite meaning—the firm generated insufficient cash to compensate for the resources committed to wealth creation.

Free cash flow is a more conventional means to measure the adequacy of cash flow. Its formula is as follows:

Free cash flows = cash flows from operations - (capital expenditures for plant and equipment + dividends paid).

The limitation of the free cash flow metric is that it is size-biased. A large firm (or division) will usually generate more free cash than a smaller firm or division. Therefore, managers should use the cash flow adequacy ratio to gauge operating performance.

Adequate cash flow adds liquidity to the firm and increases its financial flexibility. In other words, the entity increases the amount of cash it has available to take advantage of unforeseen opportunities or to address unexpected claims against cash. A cash flow adequacy of less than one reflects reductions in discretionary cash and signals diminished firm liquidity and flexibility. In those instances when the firm does not recover sufficient cash from operations, it must take one of the two following courses of action:

1. delay or postpone fixed asset purchases and dividend payments
2. find external means for financing those investments or returns on investment

The *operating (or operations) index* provides an aggregate measure of the relationship between income and operating cash flows. We compute as follows:

Operating index = cash flow from operations / income from continuing operations.

This metric should be at or near 100% because such a result signifies a high degree of correspondence between operating cash flow and earnings. Convergence indicates that the company collects its revenues in cash and pays for its expenses with cash.

Companies acquire assets and make sales to produce cash. Cash efficiency measures provide data about the extent to which they have achieved that desired effect. The cash flow return on asset ratio is the percentage of operating cash produced per invested dollar; the cash flow return on sales ratio reports cash flows from operations generated from selling goods and providing services. We calculate these ratios as follows:

Cash flows return on assets = cash flow from operations / total assets
Cash flow return on sales = cash flow from operations / revenues

One interprets these two ratios as the amount of cash the entity generates per invested dollar in resources and per sales dollar, respectively. Obviously, higher percentage returns on these two measures indicate efficient use of resources and better cash returns from revenues than lower percentages. Large returns on assets and revenues provide evidence of successful operations.

A manager analyzes past performance in order to make inferences about future wealth creation and cash flow. A firm (or division) that has historically produced enough operating cash to meet its operational needs will probably be able to do so in the future. One that has generated an excess amount of cash in the past has had financial flexibility. That result bodes well for future investment opportunities.

LIQUIDITY

Liquidity refers to an entity's ability to pay debts in the near term. Liquidity analysis, therefore, centers on current assets and current liabilities. It assesses a firm's ability to pay current obligations with cash generated from current assets. Moreover, managers consider liquidity within the context of meeting obligations without disrupting productive capabilities (e.g., selling fixed assets).

A company produces cash in the ordinary course of business by selling inventory or providing services to its customers. Creditors who contribute goods and services to those revenue-producing activities have a claim on a portion of the cash realized from sales and services. Short-term liquidity analysis determines whether an enterprise can reimburse the people and companies who contributed to the earnings process in a timely manner. Managers assess firm or divisional effectiveness in achieving that goal.

WORKING CAPITAL

Working capital is the difference between a company's current assets and its current liabilities. Managers consider it a primary liquidity indicator, and they usually calculate it first when analyzing short-term liquidity. A company whose current assets exceed its current liabilities has working capital; managers initially conclude that the firm is liquid when this condition exists. Conversely, managers initially view the firm as illiquid when current liabilities surpass current assets. Extreme Edge's working capital (in thousands of dollars) for an averaged-for-the-year 2009 is as follows: ([$360,000 + 440,000] - [$215,000 + 71,000]) = $257,000.

Managers next compute the *current (or working capital) ratio* when conducting liquidity analysis. This ratio equals current assets divided by current liabilities. The calculation for Extreme Edge's 2009 working capital ratio, on an average-for-the-year basis, as follows: $400,000 / $143,000 = 2.8:1 or, more directly, 2.8. This ratio means that Extreme Edge's current assets equaled an average of $2.80 for each dollar of current obligations during 2009 (or the company collects approximately $2.80 in cash in for each dollar it pays in maturing obligations).

A large current ratio usually indicates significant short-term liquidity or a conservative liquidity position. In general, a ratio exceeding one provides evidence that a company will be able to meet its maturing obligations. A ratio below one usually signifies short-term liquidity problems. Liquidity, however, is also a function of the following:

- Particular industry circumstances and trends within the company
- The entity's ability to sell inventory and collect receivables
- The timing of the cash inflows from those current asset conversions
- Specific payment dates of the current liabilities
- Amount of noncash current assets, such as prepaid expenses

Activity Measures

We now turn our attention to three activity ratios and their corresponding time-related measures. A current activity ratio, or turnover ratio, quantifies the number of times a liquid account turns over annually in the normal course of business. The number of days the account is outstanding before a firm sells, receives, or pays for it in cash, complements turnover activity. The following sections indicate how inventory, accounts receivable, and accounts payable activity provide liquidity insights.

Inventory turnover is the average number of times a company sells its inventory during a reporting period. We compute this ratio as follows:

Inventory turnover = cost of goods sold / average inventory

The denominator measures inventory items at their historical cost or wholesale price. Therefore, readers should use the cost of sales (wholesale or purchase price), rather than revenue (retail or selling price), as the ratio's numerator. Using cost of goods sold maintains the consistency of historical cost values in the ratio.

A more meaningful inventory activity measure than the turnover ratio is the *number of days in inventory*. It reports the average length of time an entity needs to sell its inventory. Managers compute it as follows:

Number of days in inventory = 365 days / inventory turnover

Managers interpret the quotient of this ratio as the elapsed time from the date of inventory acquisition to its point of sale. An inverse relationship exists between inventory turnover and the number of days in inventory. The higher the inventory turnover, the fewer days needed to sell inventory, and vice-versa.

The following computations and results present Extreme Edge's inventory turnover ratio (averaged-for-the year), and number of days in inventory for 2009.

- Inventory turnover = $660,000 / $225,000 = 2.93 times
- Days in inventory = 365 days / 2.93 = 124.4 days

The hypothetical e-tailer sold its inventory 2.93 times during 2009. Put another way, it took Extreme Edge an average of 124 days to sell an inventory item. For example, if the company acquired an inventory item on January 1, 2009, then it would have sold that product on May 4, 2009. Of course, some goods sell faster than 124 days and others move slower, but the mean length of time Extreme Edge holds inventory is about four months.

Accounts receivable activity measures parallel those computations made for inventory. *Accounts receivable turnover* determine the number of times receivables a firm collects cash from credit sales during the year. The *number of days in accounts receivables* reports the average length of time between a credit sale and its cash collection. We compute these two measures as follows:

> Accounts receivable turnover = sales revenues / average accounts receivable
>
> Number of days in receivables = 365 days / accounts receivable turnover

The accounts receivable activity ratios for Extreme Edge in 2009 illustrate these activity measures.

- Accounts receivable turnover = $1,200,000 / $130,000 = 9.23 times
- Number of days in receivable = 365 days / 9.23 = 39.5 days

Extreme Edge collected cash on its outstanding accounts slightly more than nine times during 2009. In other words, an average credit sale was outstanding for nearly 40 days before it was realized in cash.

Merchants and manufacturers obtain finished goods and raw materials from their vendors, respectively, in the ordinary course of business. Suppliers extend credit based on customer needs, credit history, and standard industry practices. *Accounts payable turnover* measures the annual number of vendor payments, and the *number of days in accounts payable* computes the average time required to pay for purchases. These ratios look like this:

> Accounts payable turnover = cost of goods sold / average accounts payable
>
> Number of days in payable = 365 days / accounts payable turnover

Extreme Edge's accounts payable activity ratios for 2009 are as follows:

- Accounts payable turnover = $660,000 / $105,000 = 6.29 times
- Number of days in payable = 365 days / 6.29 = 58.1 days

Extreme Edge took an average of about 58 days to pay its suppliers. For example, the company paid for an item purchased on January 1, 2009 about February 27 of that year. In the next section, we pair days in accounts payable with the other activity data discussed thus far to produce the final short-term liquidity measures.

CYCLE ANALYSIS

Managers can extend activity analysis to provide information about business operating cycles. The *inventory conversion cycle* quantifies the operating cycle. This measure sums the number of days needed to sell inventory and the number of days required to collect on the resulting receivables. The inventory conversion cycle enables managers to track the average length of time it takes to convert inventory into cash. To illustrate, refer to Extreme Edge's 2009 data for its inventory and receivable activity ratios.

Metric	Number of Days
Days in inventory	124.4
+ Days in receivables	39.5
= Inventory conversion cycle	163.9

Extreme Edge needs, on average, 164 days to convert an inventory purchase into cash. To put this amount of time into perspective, assume the company purchases inventory on January 1, 2009. They would sell that item on May 4 of that year. The e-tailer would then collect payment from the customer on June 13, 2009, or 40 days after the sale.

The *net cash conversion cycle* is the difference between the inventory conversion cycle and the number of days in accounts payable. Some refer to this metric as the *net merchandising cycle*. Managers subtract days in accounts payable from the inventory conversion cycle in order to determine net cash conversion. We now present Extreme Edge's 2009 net cash conversion data:

Metric	Number of Days
Days in inventory	124.4
+ Days in receivables	39.5
- Days in accounts payable	(58.1)
= Net cash conversion cycle	105.8

Net cash conversion cycles provide information about liquidity financing. It represents the average length of time a company needs to fund its operating activities. Cash collections lag vendor payments by 106 days in Extreme Edge's case for 2009. The company, therefore, must constantly finance three and a half months of inventory purchases.

Short-term financing correlates with the number of days in the conversion cycle—the longer the cycle the greater the need for operational financing. A negative net cash conversion cycle, on the other hand, means vendors finance working capital. Assume for the moment that Extreme Edge sells inventory every 15.6 days, instead of 124.4 days. This would reduce the company's net cash conversion cycle to negative three days (i.e., 15.6 days + 39.5 days – 58.1 days = -3). Extreme Edge would collect cash from inventory it purchased 55 days ago under this assumption, but the firm would not pay for the inventory item until day 58. In other words, Extreme Edge's vendors are financing its working capital. The company actually has the use of vendor cash for three days.

CAPITAL STRUCTURE

Capital structure relates to the amount and types of debt and equity used to finance corporate assets. The primary components of capital structure are bonds payable, long-term notes payable, preferred stock, common stock, and retained earnings. The latter three categories are equity accounts, while the first two represent creditor (or debt) financing. Companies engage assets acquired with those funds in revenue-producing activities. Those central business activities produce sufficient cash flows to add value to the enterprise, provided the firm effectively utilizes its available resources and properly structures its means of financing them. The proportion of debt to equity plays a critical role when analyzing asset financing. Capital structure analysis determines if an entity's combination of debt and equity enables wealth creation without unduly jeopardizing long-term solvency or financial flexibility.

An effective capital structure provides a firm with financial strength and stability. The proportion of debt to equity must compensate creditors for the use of their funds, provide equity investors with acceptable investment returns for the risks they incur, allow the company to take advantage of unforeseen investment opportunities, and insulate the firm from economic adversity. Managers must judge whether a firm has the right mix of long-term debt and equity financing to meet these objectives. They need an in-depth understanding of financial leverage in order to do so.

DEBT TO CAPITAL RATIOS

Managers conventionally begin an evaluation of capital structure by measuring the proportion of debt to assets financing equity. These measures compare creditor financing with total asset financing or owner-only funding. The first measure is the *total debt to total capital* (or *asset) ratio*, computed as follows:

Total debt to total capital = total liabilities / total assets

The next ratio compares *total debt to total equity*, and we calculate it as follows:

Total debt to total equity = total liabilities / total shareholders' equity

We can adjust the numerator in the first two ratios to reflect a capital structure reality. As noted, business operations require short-term creditor financing. Those claims are satisfied with cash collected on receivables and inventory sales. Therefore, we can factor those obligations out of the debt to equity ratios. The adjustment results in the *long-term debt to total capital* and *long-term to total equity* ratios:

Long-term debt to total capital = long-term liabilities / total assets
Long-term debt to total equity = long-term liabilities / total shareholders' equity

Exhibit A-3 presents Extreme Edge's 2009 debt to capital and equity ratios (averaged for the year).

Exhibit A-3
2009 Debt to Capital and Equity Ratios
(in thousands of dollars)

Ratio	Computation
Total debt to total capital	([$335 + $291]/2) / ([$780 + $835]/2) = 38.8%
Total debt to total equity	([$335 + $291]/2) / ([$445 + $544]/2) = 63.3%
Long-term debt to total capital	([$120 + $220]/2) / ([$780 + $835]/2) = 21.1%
Long-term debt to total equity	([$120 + $220]/2) / ([$445 + $544]/2) = 34.4%

A manager can gain insight about debt to investment ratios by reducing them to a dollar basis. For example, Extreme Edge's total debt to total capital ratio means that the company owes almost thirty-nine cents for every dollar used to acquire assets. Alternatively, the manager views owners as financing more than sixty-three cents of every dollar invested in corporate resources. One interprets long-term debt measures in a similar manner, except for the exclusion of current obligations.

Financial Leverage

A capital structure concern is whether the benefits derived from the borrowed funds exceed their cost. Managers calculate a financial leverage index to gauge the effectiveness of debt financing. One calculates this index by dividing return on assets into return on equity. Chapter 7 reported the *return on assets* (ROA) ratio as net income divided by total assets. *Return on equity* (ROE) equals net income divided by total shareholders' equity.

Recall from our discussions in Chapters 3 and 4 that interest on borrowed funds shields some of the firm's revenues from taxation. The deductibility of the cost of borrowed funds reduces the effective cost of debt capital. Viewed another way, it increases the firm's return on assets. We adjust the return on assets ratio by adding net interest cost to net income in the numerator of the fraction. Managers do not add back net interest charges in the return on equity calculation because shareowners ultimately bear the total cost of financing the firm.

Consider Extreme Edge's investment return data for 2009. Exhibit A-4 presents these figures along with two alternative scenarios about the cost of borrowed funds. The first assumes interest expense was $10,000, and the second assumes debt financing cost $30,000, in 2009.

Exhibit A-4
2009 Interest Expense and Net Income
(in thousands of dollars)

Income Statements	As Reported	Alternative 1	Alternative 2
Income from continuing operations	$55	$55	$55
Financial (interest) expense	20	10	30
Pretax income	35	45	25
Income tax expense (40%)	14	18	10
Net income	$21	$27	$15

Data in Exhibit A-5 presents the balance sheet impact of those earnings and the rates of return on investment for the three cases.

Exhibit A-5
Rates of Return on Assets and Equity
(in thousands of dollars)

	As Reported	Alternative 1	Alternative 2
Ending shareholders' equity	$544	$550	$538
Ending total assets	835	841	829
Return on assets (adjusted)	($21 + $12) / 835 = 4.0%	($27 + $6) / $841 = 4.0%	($15 + $18) / 829 = 4.0%
Return on equity	$21 / $544 = 3.9%	$27 / $550 = 4.9%	$15 / $538 = 2.8%
Financial leverage index	3.9 / 4.0 = .98	4.9 / 4.0 =1.2	2.8 / 4.0 = .70

Note that in the table above, adding net interest expense in the numerator consistently yields adjusted net income of $33,000. This results in approximately a 4% rate of return on assets in all the three cases. The returns on equity vary among the three cases; consequently, the financial leverage indexes vary. A manager would conclude that there is no material benefit or cost of borrowing for the reported data (i.e., an index of .98). The relatively low cost of debt financing in alternative one produces a positive financial leverage index (1.2), which signifies the advantageous use of debt financing. The high cost of debt, assumed in alternative two, diminishes corporate wealth. The cost of this debt outweighs the benefits (income) it produced.

Earnings Coverage Ratio

The earnings coverage ratio measures the extent to which a firm's operating income can meet fixed charges on borrowed funds. Managers refer to a simplified version of the earnings coverage ratio as the *times interest earned ratio*, because it reports operating earnings as a multiple of interest expense. They calculate it as follows:

Times interest earned = (pretax income + interest expense) / interest expense

or

Times interest earned = EBIT / interest expense

A high earnings coverage ratio means that the entity had little trouble paying its contractual obligations on borrowed funds. A low ratio, however, indicates difficulty in meeting those financial commitments. When the ratio is less than one, an entity has generated insufficient earnings to meet its financing charges for that reporting period. The 2009 Extreme Edge earnings coverage ratio is 2.75 ($55,000 / $20,000). In other words, the company produced $2.75 of earnings for each dollar it was obligated to pay on borrowed funds.

Appendix B

Time Value of Money Tables

Present Value of 1

N	1%	2%	3%	4%	5%	6%	7%	8%	9%	10%	11%	12%	13%
1	0.990	0.980	0.971	0.962	0.952	0.943	0.935	0.926	0.917	0.909	0.901	0.893	0.885
2	0.980	0.961	0.943	0.925	0.907	0.890	0.873	0.857	0.842	0.826	0.812	0.797	0.783
3	0.971	0.942	0.915	0.889	0.864	0.840	0.816	0.794	0.772	0.751	0.731	0.712	0.693
4	0.961	0.924	0.888	0.855	0.823	0.792	0.763	0.735	0.708	0.683	0.659	0.636	0.613
5	0.951	0.906	0.863	0.822	0.784	0.747	0.713	0.681	0.650	0.621	0.593	0.567	0.543
6	0.942	0.888	0.837	0.790	0.746	0.705	0.666	0.630	0.596	0.564	0.535	0.507	0.480
7	0.932	0.871	0.813	0.760	0.711	0.665	0.623	0.583	0.547	0.513	0.482	0.452	0.425
8	0.923	0.853	0.789	0.731	0.677	0.627	0.582	0.540	0.502	0.467	0.434	0.404	0.376
9	0.914	0.837	0.766	0.703	0.645	0.592	0.544	0.500	0.460	0.424	0.391	0.361	0.333
10	0.905	0.820	0.744	0.676	0.614	0.558	0.508	0.463	0.422	0.386	0.352	0.322	0.295
11	0.896	0.804	0.722	0.650	0.585	0.527	0.475	0.429	0.388	0.350	0.317	0.287	0.261
12	0.887	0.788	0.701	0.625	0.557	0.497	0.444	0.397	0.356	0.319	0.286	0.257	0.231
13	0.879	0.773	0.681	0.601	0.530	0.469	0.415	0.368	0.326	0.290	0.258	0.229	0.204
14	0.870	0.758	0.661	0.577	0.505	0.442	0.388	0.340	0.299	0.263	0.232	0.205	0.181
15	0.861	0.743	0.642	0.555	0.481	0.417	0.362	0.315	0.275	0.239	0.209	0.183	0.160
16	0.853	0.728	0.623	0.534	0.458	0.394	0.339	0.292	0.252	0.218	0.188	0.163	0.141
17	0.844	0.714	0.605	0.513	0.436	0.371	0.317	0.270	0.231	0.198	0.170	0.146	0.125
18	0.836	0.700	0.587	0.494	0.416	0.350	0.296	0.250	0.212	0.180	0.153	0.130	0.111
19	0.828	0.686	0.570	0.475	0.396	0.331	0.277	0.232	0.194	0.164	0.138	0.116	0.098
20	0.820	0.673	0.554	0.456	0.377	0.312	0.258	0.215	0.178	0.149	0.124	0.104	0.087
21	0.811	0.660	0.538	0.439	0.359	0.940	0.242	0.199	0.164	0.135	0.112	0.093	0.077
22	0.803	0.647	0.522	0.422	0.342	0.278	0.226	0.184	0.150	0.123	0.101	0.083	0.068
23	0.795	0.634	0.507	0.406	0.326	0.262	0.211	0.170	0.133	0.112	0.091	0.074	0.060
24	0.788	0.622	0.492	0.390	0.310	0.247	0.197	0.158	0.126	0.102	0.082	0.066	0.053
25	0.780	0.610	0.478	0.375	0.295	0.233	0.184	0.146	0.116	0.092	0.074	0.059	0.047
30	0.742	0.552	0.412	0.308	0.231	0.174	0.131	0.099	0.075	0.057	0.044	0.033	0.026
35	0.706	0.500	0.355	0.253	0.181	0.130	0.094	0.068	0.049	0.036	0.026	0.019	0.014
40	0.672	0.453	0.070	0.208	0.142	0.097	0.067	0.046	0.032	0.022	0.015	0.011	0.008
45	0.639	0.410	0.264	0.171	0.111	0.073	0.048	0.031	0.021	0.014	0.009	0.006	0.004
50	0.608	0.372	0.228	0.141	0.087	0.054	0.034	0.021	0.013	0.009	0.005	0.003	0.002

Present Value of an Annuity

N	1%	2%	3%	4%	5%	6%	7%	8%	9%	10%	11%	12%	13%
1	0.990	0.980	0.971	0.962	0.952	0.943	0.935	0.926	0.917	0.909	0.901	0.893	0.885
2	1.970	1.942	1.913	1.886	1.859	1.833	1.808	1.783	1.759	1.736	1.713	1.690	1.668
3	2.941	2.884	2.829	2.775	2.723	2.673	2.624	2.577	2.531	2.487	2.444	2.402	2.361
4	3.902	3.808	3.717	3.630	3.546	3.465	3.387	3.312	3.240	3.170	3.102	3.037	2.974
5	4.853	4.713	4.580	4.452	4.329	4.212	4.100	3.993	3.890	3.791	3.696	3.605	3.517
6	5.795	5.601	5.417	5.242	5.076	4.917	4.767	4.629	4.486	4.355	4.231	4.110	3.998
7	6.728	6.472	6.230	6.002	5.786	5.582	5.389	5.206	5.033	4.868	4.712	4.564	4.423
8	7.652	7.325	7.020	6.733	6.463	6.210	5.971	5.747	5.535	5.335	5.146	4.968	4.799
9	8.566	8.162	7.786	7.435	7.108	6.802	6.515	6.247	5.995	5.759	5.537	5.328	5.132
10	9.471	8.983	8.530	8.111	7.722	7.360	7.024	6.710	6.418	6.145	5.889	5.650	5.426
11	10.368	9.787	9.253	8.760	8.306	7.887	7.499	7.139	6.805	6.495	6.207	5.938	5.687
12	11.255	10.575	9.954	9.385	8.863	8.384	7.943	7.536	7.161	6.814	6.492	6.194	5.918
13	12.134	11.348	10.635	9.986	9.394	8.853	8.358	7.904	7.487	7.103	6.750	6.424	6.122
14	13.004	12.106	11.296	10.563	9.899	9.295	8.745	8.244	7.786	7.367	6.982	6.628	6.302
15	13.865	12.849	11.938	11.118	10.380	9.712	9.108	8.559	8.061	7.606	7.191	6.811	6.462
16	14.718	13.578	12.561	11.652	10.838	10.106	9.447	8.810	8.313	7.824	7.379	6.974	6.604
17	15.562	14.292	13.166	12.166	11.274	10.477	9.763	9.122	8.544	8.022	7.549	7.120	6.729
18	16.398	14.992	13.754	12.659	11.690	10.828	10.059	9.372	8.756	8.201	7.702	7.250	6.840
19	17.226	15.678	14.324	13.134	12.085	11.158	10.336	9.604	8.950	8.365	7.839	7.366	6.938
20	18.046	16.351	14.877	13.590	12.642	11.470	10.594	9.818	9.129	8.514	7.963	7.469	7.025
21	18.857	17.011	15.415	14.029	12.821	11.764	10.836	10.017	9.292	8.649	8.075	7.562	7.102
22	19.660	17.658	15.937	14.451	13.163	12.042	11.061	10.201	9.442	8.772	8.176	7.654	7.170
23	20.456	18.292	16.444	14.857	13.489	12.303	11.272	10.371	9.580	8.883	8.266	7.718	7.230
24	21.243	18.914	16.936	15.247	13.799	12.550	11.469	10.529	9.707	8.985	8.348	7.784	7.283
25	22.023	19.523	17.413	15.622	14.094	12.783	11.654	10.675	9.823	9.077	8.422	7.843	7.330
30	25.808	22.396	19.600	17.292	15.372	13.765	12.409	11.258	10.274	9.427	8.694	8.055	7.496
35	29.409	24.999	21.487	18.665	16.374	14.498	12.948	11.655	10.567	9.644	8.855	8.176	7.586
40	32.835	27.355	23.115	19.793	17.159	15.046	13.332	11.925	10.757	9.779	8.951	8.244	7.634
45	36.095	29.490	24.519	20.720	17.774	15.456	13.606	12.108	10.881	9.863	9.008	8.283	7.661
50	39.196	31.424	25.730	21.482	18.256	15.762	13.801	12.233	10.962	9.915	9.042	8.304	7.675

Index

LaVergne, TN USA
04 June 2010
184923LV00004B/1/P